10 Steps in Writing the Research Paper

W9-BID-161

by

Roberta H. Markman, Ph.D.
*California State College,
Long Beach, California*

and

Marie L. Waddell
*The University of Texas
at El Paso*

Revised

BARRON'S EDUCATIONAL SERIES, INC.
Woodbury, New York

© Copyright, 1971 by Barron's Educational Series, Inc.

Prior editions © Copyright, 1965 by Barron's Educational Series, Inc.

All rights reserved.
No part of this book may be reproduced
in any form, by photostat, microfilm, xerography,
or any other means, or incorporated into any
information retrieval system, electronic or
mechanical, without the written permission
of the copyright owner.

All inquiries should be addressed to
Barron's Educational Series, Inc.
113 Crossways Park Drive
Woodbury, New York 11797

Library of Congress Catalog Card No. 70-140138

International Standard Book No. 0-8120-0206-7

PRINTED IN THE UNITED STATES OF AMERICA

5 6 7 8 9 10 11 M 5 4 3

CONTENTS

Preface to the New Edition

Having seen our manual used by students for the past several years, we are delighted with the success which makes this revised edition possible. The value of these ten steps is evident from the quality of the research done by those who used this manual to guide them through the writing of their term papers. Many letters from students and instructors throughout the country further affirm the usefulness and value of such a manual.

Because one of the real advantages has been the compact format, we have kept additional materials to a minimum. There are minor changes throughout, but the major additions reflect two of our concerns: recent changes in scholarly methods and the increasing use of multi-media in literary scholarship. We have therefore taken the following steps to improve *10 STEPS:*

1. We have added some explanatory material and revised a few paragraphs for greater clarity.

2. We have added a new section on the use of the library, with information on what tools and services are available in most libraries.

3. We have added samples of documentation for such multi-media as film, tapes, phonograph recordings, casebooks, television, and radio.

4. We have changed our sample library catalogue card from the one with a Dewey-decimal system call number to one using the Library of Congress number, since most American libraries are changing to the latter.

5. We have added more information about the use of Roman numerals.
6. We have included a discussion about developing a final outline through the use of notecards.
7. We have included a special section on using the kind of in-text documentation which has become increasingly popular in recent years.
8. We have added a short section showing how to integrate documentation so that all quotations will seem relevant and the text will become more unified.
9. We have added and updated reference materials.
10. We have included an index which should help students find more rapidly certain forms needed at a particular stage of their research.

Looking forward to using the first edition in the classroom was exciting, but it is especially exciting to do this revision knowing that students and professors throughout the academic world have found this method valuable; to all of them we give heart-felt thanks for their encouragement.

Roberta Hoffman Markman
Marie Landua Waddell

HUNTINGTON HARBOUR, CALIFORNIA
FEBRUARY 1, 1971

Preface

We have attempted to present clear and complete step-by-step instructions for the writing of a research paper and to give models for all necessary research forms. Our arrangement outlines each step in the research process and puts all information concerning each step in the process together in the same section; everything about bibliography is in one section; all information about footnotes is in another, and so on. Having taught the techniques of the research paper for many years, we have often felt the need for such a book as this one.

We have attempted to write in such a way that the instructions will be simple enough for the high school student and yet complete enough for the graduate student. The experienced research writer should be able to profit from the suggested techniques and the numerous models for correct form. Even a student who has never before written a research paper should be able to follow the steps as described and write a paper with the least amount of wasted effort, the greatest amount of accuracy in form, and the assurance that his paper will be acceptable by any scholarly criterion. With the confidence which comes from the knowledge that he is following a logical and clear procedure, the student will be free to enjoy his research and to know the excitement that comes from the accomplishment of a worthwhile academic task, an accomplishment which constitutes an invaluable part of his education.

We are grateful to the students who for a decade have proved the worth of this method of research and to our many colleagues for their professional assistance and enthusiastic response to this work.

EL PASO, TEXAS

JUNE, 1962

Roberta Hoffman Markman
Marie Landua Waddell

Introduction to Research

Research is the disciplined process of investigating and seeking facts which will lead one to discover the truth about something. This truth, stated as one's thesis,* must come as a result of the facts one discovers, and it must be proved conclusively by the facts selected. The thesis may not be a statement of preconceived opinion or prejudice; the research paper may not be a stringing-together of related quotations and a collection of footnotes.

The research paper, a formal presentation of these discovered facts, provides the evidence one needs to defend the opinion he has expressed as his thesis. Consequently, one must state how and where he found these facts. If they were discovered from what other people have said or written, the student must tell who said them and where they were said so that his reader could find them also; if they were discovered by direct observation, the student must describe his experience so that his reader could repeat it and observe the same phenomena or facts. The opinion, which is the thesis, is subjectively presented; the facts, which provide the supporting points, are objectively presented.

The student learns much during the process of research. He learns to select, to evaluate, and to analyze his facts; he learns to discipline his habits of thought and work; and, most important, he learns to think: to create a new angle of vision. In this sense only, the research paper is original, but it is important enough in itself to justify the work involved in its creation.

Because nothing else so clearly reveals the true quality and merit of a student's mind, the research paper becomes a valid criterion for judging the disciplined work habits and the intellectual maturity of the student.

---

* See Research Terms Defined, pp.121–125.

The Ten Steps in Research

There is always more than one way of accomplishing any task, and doing research is no exception. After much trial and error, the experienced researcher usually arrives at some system which has proved itself to be the best for him. However the individual systems may vary, there are ten basic steps which provide a logical method for research and which result in an ease of procedure for the researcher, the ultimate economy of time and effort, the assurance that comes from following a time-tested procedure, accuracy in the result, and the most universal acceptance by examining scholars. As you proceed, you may think that you can eliminate a step or two in the process only to find later that you have created some extra ones to make up for the detour, so watch your step!

Step 1   FIND A SUBJECT.

Step 2   READ A GENERAL ARTICLE OR TWO.

Step 3   FORMULATE A TEMPORARY THESIS AND A TEMPORARY OUTLINE.

Step 4   PREPARE THE BIBLIOGRAPHY.

Step 5   TAKE NOTES FROM RELEVANT SOURCES.

Step 6   LABEL NOTECARDS; REVISE THE WORKING OUTLINE.

Step 7   WRITE THE FIRST DRAFT.

Step 8   REVISE THE TEXT; WRITE AN INTRODUCTION AND A CONCLUSION.

Step 9   FILL IN FOOTNOTES ON THE DRAFT.

Step 10   PUT THE PAPER IN ITS FINAL FORM.

FIND A SUBJECT

Finding a topic that will interest you, one that is worth your time to investigate and one for which you will have the necessary time and materials, is an extremely important step in writing the research paper. You need not be familiar with a subject before doing research on it, but you should have some interest in the general area which it involves because you will be working with that subject for a long period of time.

When the general subject is not assigned by your instructor, you can usually find one by examining your own interests, your background, or the other courses which you are studying. There are other considerations which will limit the possibilities from which you may choose.

Your choice of a suitable subject for investigation will often be determined by whether or not you are interested in reading or investigating, and consequently analyzing, the original material directly and therefore working with primary sources* or whether you are interested in investigating what others have said about your subject and therefore working with secondary sources. The usual college assignment involves the latter. Your choice will be determined further when you eliminate unsuitable subjects. Some subjects are not worth investigating; they are either too trivial, merely factual, or obviously routine. Others are often too new or current for conclusive study; a research paper must be factual, not conjectural, and must therefore be based on a variety of sources. The avail-

---

* See Research Terms Defined, pp.121–125.

ability of resource materials will vary with time and locale, so you must know your area and your library. And finally, some subjects have never been suitable for research: a biography summarized from secondary sources, the entire history of anything, or any subject which you will investigate with a closed mind.

READ A GENERAL ARTICLE

After you have decided on a subject, the next step is to read a general, authoritative article (such as one in the *Encyclopaedia Britannica* or *The Americana*) so that you can see what the possibilities and ramifications of the subject are. You will, in this first investigation, find out whether a subject is too broad to use without strict limitation or too narrow to consider at all. You will also orient yourself and become familiar with the general area in which you will be working. This reading will not only suggest ideas about how you should begin to limit your chosen, general subject but will also suggest a number of possible theses inherent in it.

Sometimes a single sentence or phrase in this article will alert your attention and suggest a question you will want to investigate. In fact, if your chosen subject is at all interesting to you, it would be almost impossible to read any general article without finding phrases or sentences which will challenge you to investigate further some aspect of that subject. Look for ideas which prompt you to ask why or how they are true, or in what specific way they may be true. These ideas will provide a basis upon which you will formulate a temporary thesis and a temporary outline (discussed under STEP 3).

If, for example, you are studying French and read a general article about France, you will find countless possibilities for research topics ranging from a comparative study of the French and American revolutions to the study of a particular influence (political, military, economic, re-

4

ligious) upon the French character. If you are studying
world literature and decide to write about Anton Chekhov
(because you once enjoyed seeing one of his plays), you
might be alerted by any of the following statements: he
contributed to the comic papers in Russia during the
1880's; he visited a convict island named Sakhalin and
wrote a book about it which effected changes in the regime
of that penal colony; his stories are developed along "cal-
culated curves"; his masterpiece, *My Life,* is filled with
symbols that give it an almost religious character. Such
statements should arouse your curiosity, make you want to
know more about some particular aspect of Chekhov's
work, and send you searching for information which might
substantiate any thesis you finally decide to develop. Certainly, such ideas should point out many fascinating paths
for you to explore.

Any time you browse through an encyclopedia, you
will find wonderful surprises and delightful reading which
may prove to be "an arch wherethro' gleams that untrav-
elled world" of knowledge and understanding which awaits
all students. Some subject you once thought or heard about,
but never had a chance to pursue, may challenge you to
look into its various implications. Even a cursory reading
of almost any general article will certainly prove that your
problem will never be one of not finding some idea to research; your only problem will be deciding which of the
myriad facets of life you will choose to investigate and then
reveal in your research project. No matter what thesis suggests itself as you read an encyclopedia article, your pursuit
of it will enable you to take a giant step toward an increased perception, awareness, and enjoyment of the all-
too-often hidden world around you.

FORMULATE A TEMPORARY THESIS AND A TEMPORARY OUTLINE

After you have found a general subject and have read a general article for background, you must next decide how you will work with the topic you have chosen. You might, for example, have selected an author as the subject of your paper. You will have access to books and articles which deal with facts about his personal life, his work, his environment, the influences on his life and work, and the significance of his influence on others. Certainly, there would be no value in simply restating the facts and opinions as you have read them; you could not retell them all, and you would have no criterion for deciding how to select those that you would retell. Consequently, you will have to decide to concentrate on some point which your preliminary reading has suggested is a truth about your topic and which further reading would probably substantiate and clarify. Just as the creative artist is led to make a final statement of truth about some aspect of life by observing and selecting from the myriad details of life's experiences, so you, as a researcher, must be able to crystallize a statement of truth by observing and selecting meaningful details from the wealth of material you will find on your topic. This truth, stated in a simple sentence, provides you with a temporary thesis. It is a statement of your opinion, a conclusion which, from what you have read, you have reason to believe is true, but which you are scholar enough to discard or alter later if you uncover facts that prove it invalid. A good thesis is never the statement of a preconceived notion or a personal prejudice which you could. prove only by distorting or ignoring facts, nor is it the statement of any indisputable fact about which further investigation would reveal nothing.

If, for example, you have decided to do your research on William Faulkner, you would not consider as a thesis a statement that he was a poor writer because you once read one of his novels which you did not enjoy (a preconceived notion), nor would you consider as a thesis a statement that he was a Southern writer (an indisputable fact). However, because you have read that his novels are sometimes difficult to read, you might consider showing that there are inconsistencies in his writing which account for the difficulty you may have experienced in reading his work; because you have read (in a general article) that he is concerned with the reconstruction of the South, you might decide to show that he sees the Old South as a strong motivating force in the lives of his characters. You may have been alerted by a statement in the general article you read that Faulkner wrote some stream-of-consciousness novels, and you may decide to investigate that technique, either its historical development or its effect on his handling of character development. Or because you have read that his vision is a tragic one, you might decide to show that William Faulkner can be considered a writer of tragedy. In other words, you will investigate one aspect of what you have read to ascertain its validity. As you question and search in your reading and note taking for the answers to your questions, you will re-evaluate your facts and modify your first opinion until you are closer to the ultimate truth, the discovery of which is always the purpose of your research.

It is important to limit your temporary thesis as soon

as possible so that, within the limits of the time in which you have to work and the assigned length of the finished paper, the truth of that thesis statement can be investigated thoroughly. The more minutely and specifically the road is marked, the more likely it is that you and your reader will reach the same destination: the realization of the truth of your thesis. No factor is more often responsible for the poor research paper than is the failure to limit a thesis. It is obvious that the less area you try to cover, the more depth you can explore and the more valuable your finished paper will be.

In working with the general thesis, for example, that some of William Faulkner's work can be considered tragedy, you would see quickly that there are too many possibilities for development in one paper because of the various interpretations of the concept of tragedy. Therefore, you might scan the material on the different concepts of tragedy to see if what you have read in the general article about Faulkner's work suggests a similarity to a particular interpretation of tragedy. Having read that Faulkner's approach manifests his interest in the psychological interpretation of character and in the new humanism, you might also find in reading a general article about Greek tragedy that Euripides manifested similar interests in his tragedies. You would now have a basis upon which to narrow and reformulate your temporary thesis. Although this thesis is necessarily a temporary one because you have not accumulated all of the available facts yet, it does provide you with an angle of vision from which you can continue your research. You now know how you are going to focus on your subject.

The particular angle of vision you have chosen will automatically suggest and determine the temporary outline you must work with. If you formulate a thesis which states that Faulkner, as a tragedian, is similar to Euripides, you would be compelled to investigate the truth of that statement (I) by finding out to what extent Faulkner is a tragedian, (II) by analyzing the characteristics of Euripides' tragedy, and (III) by considering the various aspects of Faulkner's work which show a similarity to the work of Euripides. You may not be certain that you can find any similarity, but it is obvious from the outset that these three questions, which constitute the points of your temporary outline, must be investigated before you can conclusively state your thesis as truth. Similarly, a logical analysis of any thesis that you choose to work with will suggest the points which provide your temporary outline. They outline the path through which you and your reader must travel before the statement you first wrote as a temporary thesis can be stated as a valid conclusion and become your final thesis.

With the formulation of your thesis as a temporary objective and with an outline statement of the points by which you can logically reach it, you have the necessary criteria by which, with a minimum of wasted effort, to select books for your bibliography (STEP 4) and to choose information for your notecards (STEP 5).

In setting up your temporary outline, you are actually using a deductive process. You have temporarily accepted a general statement, or premise, and you are going to investigate your sources to see whether or not that premise can be substantially supported by facts. Because a generality is completely meaningless unless it is supported by specific evidence, it is extremely important that you use the most authoritative sources available in which to find your facts. You must be wary of unsigned editorial columns or magazine articles that are not carefully documented. It is for this reason, also, that you must consult many different sources representing a wide range of thinking in order to make your paper valuable as research. However, in spite of the fact that your temporary outline is the result of a deductive process, your final thesis and outline must be inductively developed. That is, you must eventually analyze your material, or the facts accumulated, and change your temporary thesis, so that it is ultimately stated as an accurate result or conclusion of the material *you* have observed and presented. The temporary thesis, then, was the statement of a hunch or of an educated guess; the final thesis is the result of research and is a statement of truth. It is the only conclusion to which one could come from the material that *you* have selected and presented.

PREPARE THE PRELIMINARY BIBLIOGRAPHY

Why a preliminary bibliography is necessary

There are several reasons why, before you begin to do your research, it is important to prepare a preliminary bibliography even though it will include books you will never see or use.

1. You must be sure that adequate information on the subject is available to you and that your thesis is not hackneyed.

2. You must allow time to order any pertinent published materials which you may need to obtain through the inter-library loan service. There is a nominal charge for postage, and you should be prepared to wait at least a week.

3. You need to become familiar with the type of research that has been done on your topic.

4. From seeing a variety of titles, you will learn how your chosen thesis might be further limited or broadened.

5. You will be given clues about titles, subjects, and authors relating to your particular subject; for example, in looking up *Tragedy,* you might see *Aristotle,* which would lead to a definition of *Classical Tragedy,* which would lead to a definition of *Modern Tragedy,* and thence to *Krutch* and *Miller.*

Where to find a preliminary bibliography

There are many places where you will find a listing of materials that you can include in your preliminary bibliography. Of course, your bibliography will change considerably before it becomes final because many of the titles you find in your preliminary search will not be available; some will not be useful; and new sources will be added constantly as you read. Do not look in only one place for your sources. Try to investigate each of the following sections in the libraries available to you.*

1. The Card Catalogue

Check to see how the materials in your library are catalogued. Some libraries have a single catalogue in which you can look up author, title, or subject, all arranged in alphabetical order. Other libraries have a separate author catalogue in which you can locate the card for a book if you know the author's name; a second catalogue then contains alphabetized titles and subjects. Depending on your subject and your knowledge of it, you will look for books under a particular subject, a particular author, or a particular title. The author card for any book is considered the basic entry card. It is therefore important for you to know the significance of each entry on it.

---

*See The Library: pp. 116-120. See also Reference Materials and Guides, pp. 129-134.

EXAMPLE OF AN AUTHOR CARD IN THE CARD CATALOGUE

> PN1892   Sewall, Richard Benson.
> The vision of tragedy. New Haven, Yale
> University Press © 1960, © 1959,
> 178 p. 22cm.
>
> 1. Tragedy   2. Tragic, The   3. Tragedy—Hist.
> crit.   Literature—Hist. & crit.   I Title.
>
> PN1892.   S43   808.2   59—6801
> Library of Congress   62ml

NOTES:

This card, like all author cards, identifies the book by the call number* in the upper left-hand corner.

The author's name is given in inverted order; the dates of his birth and death are often included.

The first letter of the first word in each title is capitalized; but often, the entire title of the book is neither capitalized nor italicized on the catalogue card. You must remember to capitalize the first and last words and then all other words of the title except for CAP (Conjunctions, Articles, and Prepositions); also remember to underline each word of the title separately to indicate italics.

If there is a bibliography included in the book, the card will indicate it.

The Library of Congress number is the call number here; it will be at the bottom of a card using the Dewey Decimal system classification.

---

* See Library Classification Systems, pp. 126-128.

This book is catalogued also under its titles (after Roman numerals), its subjects (after the Arabic numbers), and if there were an editor and a translator they would be also listed after Roman numerals. The Dewey Decimal call number follows the Library of Congress number at the bottom.

The way in which any book is catalogued or cross-filed will suggest other possible subjects for you to investigate.

2. Periodical Indexes

These will list magazine articles published on your subject; some of the most important indexes are listed below.

a. *The Reader's Guide to Periodical Literature* will list articles published in American magazines since 1900. It is a subject and author index with cross references; however, the subject index is the more complete.

> NOTE: You will have to look in the volume for each year in which articles on your subject could have been written; for example, you would not look up *atomic energy* in the 1930 volume, but you would look up *tragedy* in every volume.
>
> Do not put the information on your bibliography card the way it appears in *The Reader's Guide*. The abbreviations are explained at the front of each volume. The entry in the 1919-1921 volume which appears thus:
>
> Notes on tragedy. L. Lewisohn. Nation 108:879-80 My 31 '19
>
> will be translated to a bibliography card thus:

Lewisohn, L.
"Notes on Tragedy,"
The Nation,
May 31, 1919,
pp. 879-80.

b. *Social Science and Humanities Index* (1907 to date) covers many learned and professional journals not included in *The Reader's Guide,* and it lists foreign as well as American periodicals. It is extremely valuable for articles published since 1907.

c. *Poole's Index to Periodical Literature* is a subject index to British and American magazine articles published from 1802-1906.

d. *Nineteenth Century Reader's Guide to Periodical Literature* (1890-1899) is an index to fifty-one periodicals from 1890-1899. It gives the subject, author, and illustrator; some works of literature are listed under title entries. A special feature is the identification (wherever possible) of articles published anonymously.

e. *Book Review Digest* (1905 to date) gives reports on contemporary reviews and brief but useful information about the worth of books. There are excerpts from many of the reviews cited.

f. M.L.A. *Bibliographies* (1921 to present) are yearly volumes listing essays in various periodicals devoted to language and literature (English, American, French, Spanish, Italian, German).

3. Special Indexes

These include listings of books and magazines and newspaper articles on a variety of special subjects (such as education, religion, art, book reviews, medicine, engineering, biographies) and are usually found on open reference-room shelves. For example,

The New York Times Index classifies all of the *Times* articles. It gives the date on which an event occurred, making it easier for you to look up information in other newspapers; its obituaries contain valuable biographical material about prominent people.

Essay and General Literature Index lists more of the scholarly magazine articles on more sophisticated subjects than *The Reader's Guide.*

PMLA (the journal called *Publications of the Modern Language Association*) has an index in each May issue.

4. Bibliographies

There are many publications which are themselves merely bibliographies. Some are compiled on particular subjects; others, on a particular person and his work. For example,

Murphey, Robert W., *How and Where to Look It Up,* (1958), divides his bibliography by subject; under each subject he lists general encyclopedias and almanacs, guides to periodicals, literary indexes, guides to reference works, government pamphlets, dictionaries, biographical material, and other kinds of sources which are available for each subject listed. He also has a chapter on how to use the library and a chapter with hints on research writing.

> Winchell, Constance M. *Guide to Reference Books*, 8th ed., lists general works, bibliographies, periodicals, dissertations, indexes, encyclopedias, dictionaries, biographies on various subjects.

There are more indexes listed on pp. 131–134.

5. Special Encyclopedias

> Many of these include excellent bibliographies in addition to the articles on particular subjects. For example, you will find bibliographies at the end of most articles in the *Encyclopaedia Britannica*. Check the card catalogue for encyclopedias on special subjects, such as art, American history, American government, religion, physics, music, and so forth.

6. Sources Which You Use

> In most of your sources you will find clues to other relevant material by looking either in a bibliography at the back, in the footnotes, or in the material itself.

How to write your bibliography cards

Record each entry or source on a separate 3″ x 5″ index card.

Record the name of the author, the title, and the facts of publication accurately. The card, not the book, will be the source of information for the data you will use later in writing the footnotes and the final bibliography.

In order to save time and effort, you should make up your cards with whatever information you have, leaving lines and spaces to be completed when you have the actual book or other source in your hands.

On the back of the bibliography card put the call number

and/or the place where you found out about this source. Also put any other information to which you might want to refer later.

There are only two basic bibliographical forms:

1. There is a basic form for a source with its own title.

2. There is a basic form for an article contained within a larger work.

Form for a source with its own title

(*Note: You need not have used or read the entire work.*)

```
Sewall, Richard B.
The Vision of Tragedy.
New Haven:  Yale University Press,
1959.
```

1st line: author's name in inverted order

(If there are two or more authors, use the form in example 1 or 2 below.)

end punctuation: period

2nd line: title of book

(Capitalize the first and last word and all other words except CAP—short Conjunctions, Articles, and short Prepositions; underline each word separately to indicate title as it appears on outside of book; underlining is a substitute for italics.)

end punctuation: period

3rd line: facts of publication

There are three acceptable forms:

a. place of publication followed by colon and name of publisher;

b. name of publisher followed by comma and place of publication;

c. place of publication only; this form is neither as logical nor as helpful to the reader as the other two because someone wanting the book would not get it by writing to New Haven.

end punctuation for all forms: comma

NOTES: You must choose one of the three forms and use it consistently.

You must write the name of the publisher exactly as it appears on the title page, abbreviating and capitalizing only those words that are abbreviated and/or capitalized.

If more than one place of publication is given, use the first one listed unless it is in a foreign country; if only a foreign country is given, use it.

If the publisher is not given, write the abbreviation in brackets thus: [n.p.].

If the place of publication is not given, write the abbreviation in brackets thus: [n.p.].

4th line: date of publication

(Whenever more than one date of publication or copyright is given, use the most recent one. If no date is given, write the abbreviation in brackets thus: [n.d.].)

end punctuation: period

Models for a source with its own title

1. two authors

Campbell, Harry Modean, and Ruel E. Foster.
William Faulkner: A Critical Appraisal.
Norman: University of Oklahoma Press,
1951.

2. more than two authors

Bachelor, Joseph M., and others.
Current Thinking and Writing, 3rd series.
New York: Appleton-Century-Crofts,
1956.

NOTE: The author line may be thus:
Bachelor, Joseph M., *et al.*

3. an editor in addition to an author (collected works of one author with editor)

Wordsworth, William.
The Prelude or Growth of a Poet's Mind.
Ernest de Selincourt, ed.
New York: Oxford University Press,
1947.

4. an editor, but no author

Gwynn, Frederick L., and Joseph L.
 Blotner, eds.
Faulkner in the University.
Charlottesville: University of Virginia
 Press,
1959.

> NOTE: A compiler would be treated the same as an
> editor: his name followed by the abbrevia-
> tion (comp.) for *compiler*.

5. a translator

Decharmé, Paul.
Euripides and the Spirit of His Dramas.
Trans. James Loeb.
New York: Macmillan,
1906.

6. an author, a translator, and an editor

Euripides.
Bacchae,
trans. Henry Birkhead.
Ten Greek Plays in Contemporary Translations,
L. R. Lind, ed.
Boston: Houghton Mifflin,
1957.
Pp. 325-64.

NOTE: Page numbers are included because the particular play which was read can be found on these pages only. *P* is capitalized because it comes after a period. On card number 5 the abbreviation for *translator* is capitalized because it follows a period; on card number 6 it follows a comma and is therefore not capitalized. Birkhead translated only this particular play in the collection.

7. an editor, but no author (not an anthology)

Great Dialogues of Plato.
Trans. W. H. D. Rouse.
Eric H. Warmington and Philip G. Rouse, eds.
New York: The New American Library of World
 Literature, Inc.,
1956.

8. a book in a series edited by one other than the author

Malstrom, Vincent H., and Ruth M. Malstrom.
Norway in the "Life in Europe" series,
Raymond E. Fideler and others, eds.
Grand Rapids, Michigan: Fideler Company,
1955.

NOTE: If the volumes were numbered, the second line would be thus:

Norway, Vol. XV of the "Life in Europe" series, and the other lines, the same as already indicated.

9. no author

```
Time, Talent, and Teachers.
New York:  The Ford Foundation,
1960.
```

10. a book with a subtitle or secondary title

```
Hopper, Vincent F., trans. and ed.
Chaucer's Canterbury Tales:  An Interlinear
 Translation.
Woodbury, New York:  Barron's Educational
 Series,
1970.
```

NOTE: Obviously Chaucer did not write a book with this title; therefore this entry is correct for this book. If you quoted the introduction by Dr. Hopper, you would use this card for bibliography and for footnote. If you quoted the lines from Chaucer with the older spelling, your card would be thus:

10a.

```
Chaucer, Geoffrey.
"The Pardoner's Tale," in
Chaucer's Canterbury Tales:  An Interlinear
 Translation.
Vincent F. Hopper, ed.
Woodbury, New York:  Barron's Educational
 Series,
1970.
```

11. one volume only of a multi-volume set when each volume has a separate title

Parrington, Vernon Louis.
The Romantic Revolution in America,
  1800-1860.
Vol. II of Main Currents in American Thought.
  3 vols.
New York: Harcourt, Brace,
1930.

12. one volume in a multi-volume set when all volumes have the same title

Euripides.
Orestes,
trans. E. P. Coleridge.
Vol. II of The Complete Greek Drama,
Whitney J. Oates and Eugene O'Neill Jr,
  eds. 2 vols.
New York: Random House,
1938.
Pp. 111-70.

13. corporate authorship

Committee on College Teaching.
College Teaching as a Career.
Washington, D. C.: American Council on
  Education,
1958.

14. a government document

U. S., Congressional Record,
80th Cong., 2nd Sess., 1948,
XCII, Part 6, 5539.

15. a pamphlet, bulletin, or manual

Downer, Alan.
Recent American Drama (no. 7 in a series of
 University of Minnesota Pamphlets on Ameri-
 can Writers).
Minneapolis: University of Minnesota Press,
1961.

NOTE: Omit parenthetical entry if the pamphlet is
not one of a series.

16. a book in a series all written by the same author

Wood, William.
Elizabethan Sea-Dogs
(The Chronicles of America Series).
New Haven: Yale University Press,
1918.

NOTE: The form here is a different version of example 15 above; both are correct.

17. **an anthology considered as a whole**
    (see p. 31 #3 for individual article in an anthology)

```
Locke, Louis G., and others, eds.
Toward Liberal Education, 4th ed.
New York:  Holt, Rinehart and Winston,
1962.
```

18. **dictionary**

```
The American Heritage DICTIONARY of the
 English Language.
New York:  Houghton Mifflin,
1969.
```

19. **record or tape**

```
Lerner, Alan Jay, and Frederick Loewe.
My Fair Lady.
Columbia Masterworks,
OS2015.
```

20. **movie**

```
Shakespeare, William.
Romeo and Juliet.
Franco Zeffirelli, director-producer.
Paramount Pictures, 1968.
```

21. radio program

```
Fuller, Jason Joe.
"Forecast for the Future."
Radio broadcast, KTAM,
Phoenix, January 30, 1970.
```

22. television program

```
Room 222  (ABC series):
"Once Upon a Time There Was Air You
 Couldn't See."
KABC (Channel 7) Los Angeles,
January 28, 1970.
```

Form for a source contained within a larger work

```
Bowling, Lawrence Edward.
"Faulkner and the Theme of Innocence,"
Kenyon Review,
Summer, 1958,
pp. 466-87.
```

1st line: author's name in reverse order

> (For two or more authors, see examples 1 and 2 in the section above.)

end punctuation: period

2nd line: title of the article, essay, or poem (the contained work) **capitalized and enclosed in quotation marks**

end punctuation: comma before the closing quotation marks

> (If there is punctuation as part of the title, enclose that punctuation within the quotation marks as part of the title and omit your comma.)

3rd line: title of the larger work in which the article appears

> (The title is underlined, one word at a time, and capitalized except for CAP—short Conjunctions, Articles, and short Prepositions.

> The title is followed by a comma; if your instructor insists on a volume number, give it in Roman numerals alone (without the abbreviation for *volume*), followed by a comma.

end punctuation: comma (if no parentheses will follow on line 4)

no comma (if parentheses will follow on line 4)

4th line: the date of publication followed by a comma:
October 22, 1970,

> OR if you put a volume number on line 3, then put parentheses around the date with a comma after the closing mark:
> (October 22, 1970),

5th line: the pages on which the particular article can be
found

(If line 3 had a volume given, omit the abbreviation p. or pp.; if no volume is given on line 3, there
will be no parentheses on line 4 and you will use
the abbreviations p. or pp.)

end punctuation: period

(To give the pages on which an article occurs, use

p. 12 to indicate that the article is complete on
one page;

pp. 11-19 to indicate that the article covers nine
pages;

pp. 11-19, 36 to indicate that after the first nine
pages, the article continues on p. 36;

pp. 11-19, 36-40 to indicate that after the first
nine pages, the article continues from
pages 36 to 40.)

Models for a Source Contained Within a Larger Work

1. an encyclopedia article

Murray, George G. Aimé.
"Greek Drama: Origins,"
Encyclopaedia Britannica (1958),
VII, 578-80.

NOTES: Most articles are signed with only the initials of the author; at the front of the first
volume is a section listing the initials and
full names and credentials of the contribu-

tors. This is probably the only type of listing in which a writer named Adam Zargos would be listed *before* Zelda Adams.

For an unsigned article, you would write nothing on the first line above the title of the article but leave the line blank; you may find the author's name later.

Encyclopedias reverse titles, particularly names, in order to list articles alphabetically; you may or may not, but be consistent.

2. a newspaper article or an editorial, signed

```
Miller, Arthur.
"Tragedy and the Common Man,"
The New York Times,
February 27, 1949,
II, pp. 1, 3.
```

NOTE: For an unsigned article, you would write nothing on the top line;

the date is not in parentheses because there is no volume number;

the last line indicates that the article is in section II, page 1, continued on page 3 of the paper.

3. an essay (or other article) written by one person in an
   anthology edited by another

Orwell, George.
"Politics and the English Language,"
The Pursuit of Learning.
Nathan Comfort Starr, ed.
New York: Harcourt, Brace,
1956.
Pp. 46-56.

4. an introduction or a limited part of a book by one
   other than the author

Collins, Carvel.
"About the Sketches," an introduction to
William Faulkner, New Orleans Sketches.
New York: Grove Press,
1961.
Pp. 9-34.

5. **magazine article with no author** (See note below if author is known.)

```
"10 Amazing Years:  1947-1957."
U.S. News & World Report,
December 27, 1957,
pp. 42-53.
```

NOTE: A magazine article with an author would be identical to this form, but the author's name would go on the line above the title.

6. **the author of part of a book in a series edited by others**

```
Arrowsmith, William.
"Introduction to Hecuba,"
Euripides.  Vol. III of The Complete Greek
  Tragedies,
David Grene and Richmond Lattimore, eds.
Chicago:  The University of Chicago Press,
1959.
Pp. 489-92.
```

NOTE: For volume on line 3, MLA suggests either III, Vol. III, or No. 3.

7. **casebook** (controlled research)

```
Stevenson, David.
"J. D. Salinger:  The Mirror of Crisis,"
Nation,
March 9, 1957,
Pp. 215-217, in
If You Really Want To Know:  A CATCHER
 Casebook.
Malcolm M. Marsden, ed.
Chicago:  Scott, Foresman,
1963.
Pp. 22-25.
```

NOTE: There are two ways to use a casebook: as an anthology of essays about a particular subject or as a library containing essays which you will read and document as if you were reading the original. For the latter use, the original pagination appears in the casebook with slash marks wherever a page change occurred in the original. Check with your instructor about how he wants you to use the casebook, but it would never be wrong to use the form above.

8. **a reprint with critical comment by editor**

```
Wright, Andrew.
"Afterword," in
Joyce Cary, The Horse's Mouth.
London, 1944;
rpt. New York:
Perennial Library ed. - Harper & Row,
1965.
Pp. 347-353.
```

FORM FOR SPECIAL PROBLEMS

1. mimeographed material

Warren, Robert Penn.
"William Faulkner and His South."
The University of Virginia: transcript of
  the First Peter Rushton Seminar in Contem-
  porary Prose and Poetry and the sixteenth
  in the series sponsored by the Schools of
  English,
March 31, 1951.   (Mimeographed.)

NOTE: This form may be altered and used to make
        a bibliography card for unpublished
        speeches.

2. unpublished thesis or dissertation

Micules, Leonard.
"The Road to William Faulkner."
Unpublished Ph.D. dissertation,
Dept. of English, University of California
  at Los Angeles,
1957.

3. published lecture

Faulkner, William.
"Never Be Afraid" (Speech given at Oxford
 Mississippi High School Commencement),
The Harvard Advocate,
November, 1951,
p.7.

4. unpublished lecture

Sonnichsen, Dr. C. Leland.
Class lecture on Southwestern literature.
Texas Western College, El Paso, Texas,
April 10, 1962.

5. abridgment

Style Manual (abridged), rev. ed.
Washington: Government Printing Office,
1959.

6. **The Bible or any well-known literary work which can be identified by book or scene plus lines or by chapter and verse**

> I Corinthians.
> The Bible.
> Revised Standard Version,
> 1952.

NOTE: The names of books of sacred scripture are neither underlined nor put in quotation marks. The translation of the Bible is assumed to be the King James Version unless another is named, as in the example above.

6a.

> Milton, John.
> Paradise Lost.
> Book I.

NOTE: The particular edition you used is not needed unless the work is a translation.

The name of a novel or a long poem would be underlined even if it is part of an anthology.

7. book review without title

Beach, Joseph Warren.
Review of <u>Henry James</u>:   <u>The Major Phase</u>,
by F. O. Matthiessen.
<u>American Literature</u>,
March, 1945,
pp. 93-95.

NOTE: If this had had a title, it would be given in quotation marks on the line after the name of the reviewer, Beach; the entry would then continue as above.

8. letters

Hemingway, Ernest.
A letter to Roberta Hoffman, dated August 12,
1957, New York, and now in the archives of
The University of Texas at El Paso Library,
El Paso, Texas.

NOTE: In a footnote, simply: Unpublished letter from Ernest Hemingway to Roberta Hoffman, dated August 12, 1957.

9. interview

Leach, Dr. Joseph L.
Personal interview on style.
El Paso, Texas,
June 25, 1962.

10. an editorial, unsigned or signed

Editorial in The El Paso (Texas) Times,
July 3, 1962, p. 5.

NOTE: If the newspaper includes the word *the* in the masthead, you would include it in the title; otherwise, you would not. If the paper is internationally known, you need not add the name of the city, state, or country.

If the editorial is signed, simply write the name of the author on the line above the title of the editorial.

11. record jacket information.

The Bitter and the Sweet,
Peter Seeger.
Columbia Records, 1962.
CS 8716.

NOTE: If the writing on the jacket is signed, add the
name on the first line.

To quote from any single band or song on
the record, enter the information as for an
anthology.

12. a pamphlet included with a record

Kostelanetz, Richard, and the
Editors of Time-Life Records.
"A Listener's Guide to the Recordings,"
The Music of Today in "The Story of
 Great Music" series.
Time-Life Records. STL 145.
New York: Time Incorporated, 1967.

13. a lecture on a record or tape

Scherman, Thomas, narrator and conductor.
"Musical Program Notes,"
Beethoven's Symphony No. 5 in C Minor,
 Op. 67.
Sir Adrian Boult conducting The Phil-
harmonic Promenade Orchestra of London.
Vanguard, MARS 3005.

How to prepare the final bibliography (to be done as part of step 10)

1. Take out all the bibliography cards to which you have referred in your footnotes. These cards constitute your working bibliography and are the only ones which will be used in making your final bibliography.

2. The number of sources you will list on the final bibliography should equal the number of first-entry footnotes in your paper. (These are the footnotes which give full bibliographical information the first time you document material from a source.)

3. Alphabetize your working bibliography cards according to the first letter that appears on the card, excepting *a, an,* and *the.* (The first letter may be in the author's name, the title of a magazine article, and so forth.) If the title begins with a Roman numeral, alphabetize according to the word that follows the Roman numeral; if the first word in the title is an Arabic number, alphabetize according to the way that number would be spelled. For example, "X Steps" would be alphabetized under *S,* but "10 Steps" would be alphabetized under *T.*

4. Since the bibliography page is a title page, the title, BIBLIOGRAPHY, is centered and typed in capitals without underlining, and the page number is centered at the bottom of the page; it may be enclosed by parentheses or dashes.

5. The bibliography entries are single-spaced within each entry and double-spaced between entries. Write as a continuous sentence; do not divide into lines as on the cards. The second and subsequent lines of each entry are indented as for a paragraph (5 spaces); the punctuation on the bibliography card is copied exactly.

6. Bibliography entries are never numbered. Ordinarily, the bibliography is not divided into types of sources.

BIBLIOGRAPHY*

The American College Dictionary. New York: Random House, 1960.

Aristotle. Natural Science. Philip Wheelwright, trans. and ed. Garden City, New York: Doubleday, Doran, 1935.

Arrowsmith, William. "Introduction to Hecuba," Euripides. Vol. III of The Complete Greek Tragedies, David Grene and Richmond Lattimore, eds. Chicago: The University of Chicago Press, 1959. Pp. 489-92.

Bachelor, Joseph M., and others. Current Thinking and Writing, 3rd series. New York: Appleton-Century-Crofts, 1956.

Beach, Joseph Warren. Review of Henry James: The Major Phase, by F. O. Matthiessen. American Literature, March, 1945, pp. 93-95.

Bowling, Lawrence Edward. "Faulkner and the Theme of Innocence," Kenyon Review, Summer, 1958, pp. 466-87.

Campbell, Harry Modean, and Ruel E. Foster. William Faulkner: A Critical Appraisal. Norman: University of Oklahoma Press, 1951.

Chaucer, Geoffrey. "The Pardoner's Tale," in Chaucer's Canterbury Tales: An Interlinear Translation. Vincent F. Hopper, ed. Woodbury, New York: Barron's Educational Series, Inc., 1961.

Collins, Carvel. "About the Sketches," an introduction to William Faulkner, New Orleans Sketches. New York: Grove Press, 1961. Pp. 9-34.

21

---

* This is a sample bibliography compiled from the sample bibliography cards shown on the preceding pages.

NOTE: All of these sources are reproduced as footnotes beginning on page 81.

22

Committee on College Teaching. College Teaching as a Career.
    Washington, D.C.: American Council on Education, 1958.

I Corinthians. The Bible. Revised Standard Version, 1952.

Decharme, Paul. Euripides and the Spirit of His Dramas.
    Trans. James Loeb. New York: Macmillan, 1906.

Downer, Alan. Recent American Drama (No. 7 in a series of
    University of Minnesota Pamphlets on American Writers).
    Minneapolis: University of Minnesota Press, 1961.

Editorial in The El Paso (Texas) Times, July 3, 1962, p. 5.

Euripides. Bacchae, trans. Henry Birkhead. Ten Greek Plays
    in Contemporary Translations, L. R. Lind, ed. Boston:
    Houghton Mifflin, 1957. Pp. 325-64.

*_____. Orestes, trans. E. P. Coleridge. Vol. II of The
    Complete Greek Drama, Whitney J. Oates and Eugene O'Neill
    Jr., eds. 2 vols. New York: Random House, 1938.
    Pp. 111-70.

Faulkner, William. "Never Be Afraid" (Speech given at Oxford
    Mississippi High School Commencement), The Harvard
    Advocate, November, 1951, p. 7.

Fuller, Jason Joe. "Forecast for the Future." Radio broadcast,
    KTAM, Phoenix, January 30, 1970.

Great Dialogues of Plato. Trans. W. H. D. Rouse. Eric H.
    Warmington and Philip G. Rouse, eds. New York: The New
    American Library of World Literature, Inc., 1956.

Gwynn, Frederick L., and Joseph L. Blotner, eds. Faulkner
    in the University. Charlottesville: University of
    Virginia Press, 1959.

---

* This line indicates that the author for this entry is the same as for the
entry immediately above. Underline seven spaces before the period.

23

Hemingway, Ernest. A letter to Roberta Hoffman, dated
     August 12, 1957, New York, and now in the archives of
     Texas Western College Library, El Paso, Texas.

Hopper, Vincent F., trans. and ed. Chaucer's Canterbury Tales:
     An Interlinear Translation. Woodbury, New York: Barron's
     Educational Series, Inc., 1961.

Kostelanetz, Richard, and the Editors of Time-Life Records. "A
     Listener's Guide to the Recordings," The Music of Today
     series. Time-Life Records. STL 145. New York: Time
     Incorporated, 1967.

Leach, Dr. Joseph L. Personal interview on style. El Paso,
     Texas, June 25, 1962.

Lerner, Alan Jay, and Frederick Loewe. My Fair Lady. Columbia
     Masterworks, S2015.

Lewishon, L. "Notes on Tragedy," The Nation, May 31, 1919,
     pp. 879-80.

Locke, Louis G., and others, eds. Toward Liberal Education,
     4th ed. New York: Holt, Rinehart and Winston, 1962.

Malstrom, Vincent H., and Ruth M. Malstrom. Norway in
     the "Life in Europe" series, Raymond E. Fideler and
     others, eds. Grand Rapids, Michigan: Fideler Company,
     1955.

Micules, Leonard. "The Road to William Faulkner." Unpub-
     lished Ph.D. dissertation, Department of English,
     University of California at Los Angeles, 1957.

Miller, Arthur. "Tragedy and the Common Man," The New York
     Times, February 27, 1949, II, pp. 1, 3.

Milton, John. Paradise Lost. Book I, 11. Pp. 105-124.

24

Murray, George G. Aime. "Greek Drama: Origins." Encyclopaedia
    Britannica (1958), VII, pp. 578-80.

Orwell, George. "Politics and the English Language," The
    Pursuit of Learning. Nathan Comfort Starr, ed. New
    York: Harcourt, Brace, 1956. Pp. 46-56.

Parrington, Vernon Louis. The Romantic Revolution in
    America, 1800-1860. Vol. II of Main Currents in
    American Thought. 3 vols. New York: Harcourt,
    Brace, 1930.

Record jacket information. The Bitter and the Sweet, Peter Seeger.
    Columbia Records, 1962. CS 8716.

Shakespeare, William. Romeo and Juliet. Franco Zeffirelli,
    director-producer. Paramount Pictures, 1968.

Room 222 (ABC series): "Once Upon a Time There Was Air You
    Couldn't See." KABC (Channel 7) Los Angeles, January 28,
    1970.

Scherman, Thomas, narrator and conductor. "Musical Program
    Notes," Beethoven's Symphony No. 5 in C Minor, Op. 67.
    Sir Adrian Boult conducting The Philharmonic Promenade
    Orchestra of London. Vanguard, MARS 3005.

Sewall, Richard B. The Vision of Tragedy. New Haven:
    Yale University Press, 1959.

Sonnichsen, Dr. C. Leland. Class lecture on Southwestern
    literature. Texas Western College, El Paso, Texas,
    April 10, 1962.

Stevenson, David. "J. D. Salinger: The Mirror of Crisis,"
    Nation, March 9, 1957, in If You Really Want to Know:
    a CATCHER Casebook, Malcolm M. Marsden, ed. Chicago:
    Scott, Foresman and Company, 1963.

25

Style Manual (abridged), rev. ed. Washington: Government
        Printing Office, 1959.

"10 Amazing Years: 1947-1957." U. S. News & World Report,
        December 27, 1957, pp. 42-53.

Time, Talent, and Teachers. New York: The Ford Foundation,
        1960.

U. S., Congressional Record, 80th Cong., 2nd Sess., 1948,
        XCII, Part 6, p. 5539.

Warren, Robert Penn. "William Faulkner and His South." The
        University of Virginia: transcript of the First Peter
        Rushton Seminar in Contemporary Prose and Poetry and
        the sixteenth in the series sponsored by the schools of
        English, March 31, 1951. (Mimeographed.)

Wood, William. Elizabethan Sea-Dogs (The Chronicles of
        America Series). New Haven: Yale University Press,
        1918.

Wordsworth, William. The Prelude or Growth of a Poet's
        Mind. Ernest de Selincourt, ed. New York: Oxford
        University Press, 1947.

Wright, Andrew. "Afterword," in Joyce Cary, The Horse's
        Mouth. London, 1944; rpt. New York: Perennial Library
        ed. - Harper & Row, 1965. Pp. 347-353.

TAKE NOTES
FROM RELEVANT SOURCES

Good notecards are the key to a well-developed, easy-to-read paper and will facilitate the actual writing of your paper. In fact, to a great extent, the notecards actually determine the course of your research and the final paper you will write.

The order in which you take notes will not be the order in which you will use them in your paper; therefore, it is important to keep them independent of each other and clear in meaning to you. Each notecard must be precisely identified as to source and page so that you can document the information if you use it in your paper; or if you are working with sources that are not printed matter, be sure to indicate how and where you obtained your information.

The amount and kind of information you write on each card will vary with the type of note you take, which will be guided not only by the information you record but also by the way you think it might be used in your paper. (The section marked KINDS OF NOTECARDS, pp. 51 to 62 will indicate possible varieties.) Follow the procedure outlined below and your note taking will be orderly and rewarding.

How to take notes

1. Write your notes in ink on 4″ x 6″ cards; some instructors may prefer the 3″ x 5″ size.

2. Write on one side of the card only; never continue a note on to a second card.

3. Before you take a single note from any source, take out the bibliography card that you have prepared for that source. Check each item of the bibliography card against the source in your hands to make sure that you have the complete and correct facts concerning that particular source. Fill in any information you did not already have on the card.

4. Write an identifying letter-symbol very clearly on your bibliography card in the lower right-hand corner. This letter will identify that particular source as you take notes from it; see the example on the bibliography card below (p. 49), and on all of the notecards which follow page 50. Be sure not to use any letter twice; only one bibliography card will be marked A, for example, but many notecards may be from the source you identify as A. Go through the alphabet, but do not use the letters I and O as they could look too much like page numbers. If you have more than 24 sources, double the letters (AA or BB) or add a number (A1, B1), the second time around.

It is a good idea to keep the bibliography card at hand while you take notes from the source it identifies. Then you can be sure that the letter-symbol you enter in the upper left-hand corner of each notecard matches the one on the bibliography card. On a separate "safety sheet" and in a different place, you should keep an alphabetical list of these letters with the complete bibliographical data which each identifies.

REMEMBER: The A, B, C symbols will not indicate the order in which you will later list your bibliography (that order will be determined by the first word on the bibliography card) nor will the letters indicate the order in which you take notes or later use the note-cards.

NOTE: Many authorities suggest that the author's name be used to identify the source of the notes; others suggest that the abbreviated title be used, and still others prefer that both the title and the author be written on each notecard. However, each of these methods would involve much more time than the use of the identifying letters, and each entails a possible confusion if more than one book or article is written by the same man or has a similar title.·

The use of the identifying letter saves much time in inserting documentation on the first draft (see STEP 7), avoids possible confusion of sources, and provides the student with the evidence that every bibliography card so identified has been handled and checked for accuracy of bibliographical data.

5. Write only one idea from one source on each card; never use a single card for notes from two sources.

6. Before you begin to write your notes, be sure to identify the source. In the upper left-hand corner above the top line, write the letter or symbol which identifies the particular source you are now reading. Reserve the rest of the top line for the outline label or slug. See STEP 6.

   Put the page number in a circle before the first word on the notecard. If one idea is discussed on several pages in the source, indicate each page change by encircling the new page number before writing down the first word taken from that page. For example: (36) "There are several factors. . . . (37) The first factor . . . and (40) the second factor are important."

7. Early in your reading you will discover the need to adjust your reading speed to fit the material; not all printed material will be of equal value to you. When Bacon wrote that "some books are to be tasted, others

to be swallowed, and some few to be chewed and digested," he could have been writing instructions to the student engaged in research. You must determine the relevance of each new source to your thesis and then decide how you will read it and what notes or information you need to take from it.

8. When you find information which you want, decide which kind of note will suit your needs. Use symbols, signs, and abbreviations to save time in writing the note. Experienced researchers take various kinds of notes, samples of which follow the reproduced sample source page from which all notes in this section are taken.

9. When you are about half-way through your notetaking, see STEP 6 before continuing to take notes.

10. Do not hesitate to take duplicating or contradictory notes; you may need them to defend your thesis later or to have a choice of sources to quote.

NOTE: On each sample notecard in this section, A is the symbol identifying the Master's thesis by Hoffman as the source from which all notes are taken.

Below is the sample bibliography card for that thesis, completed as it would appear when the symbol has been added:

```
Hoffman, Roberta G.
"Tragedy:  from Athens to Yoknapatawpha."
Unpublished Master's thesis,
Department of English, Columbia University,
1961.


                      A
```

The Preface reproduced below is the source for the sample notecards given in the following section.

PREFACE

Two of the novels of William Faulkner, The Sound and the Fury and Light in August, have provided for me, as for many other readers, a tremendous stimulus for thought. After a rudimentary study of Faulkner, I felt compelled to make a study of his best novels. Knowing the characteristics of classical tragedy, I could not read these novels without an awareness of their basic similarity to the tragic form in spite of the idea that Joseph Wood Krutch expresses to the contrary in "The Tragic Fallacy"[1] concerning the inability of modern writers to create tragedy because of their lack of tragic faith. It seemed obvious to me that Arthur Miller's concept, expressed in "Tragedy and the Common Man," which recognizes the need for tragedy to be concerned with "the heart and spirit of the average man,"[2] provided enough reason to the contrary to permit me to substantiate an argument for the existence of tragedy in the twentieth century. Furthermore, I was convinced that the best prose of William Faulkner qualified him as a modern tragedian.

---

[1]Joseph Wood Krutch, "The Tragic Fallacy," The Modern Temper: A Study and a Confession (New York: Harcourt, Brace and Co., 1956), pp. 79-97.

[2]Arthur Miller, "Tragedy and the Common Man," The New York Times, February 27, 1949, II, 3, states that "there is a misconception of tragedy. . . . It is the idea that tragedy is of necessity allied to pessimism. . . . In truth tragedy implies more optimism in its author than does comedy . . . (and) ought to be the reinforcement of the onlooker's brightest opinions of the human animal."

Roberta G. Hoffman, "Tragedy: from Athens to Yoknapatawpha" (unpublished Master's thesis, Department of English, Columbia University, 1961), p. iv.

Kinds of notecards

All notes for the following illustrations are taken from the preface reproduced on the preceding page. That Preface is part of the Master's thesis which is identified on the bibliography card given on page 49 and labeled A; therefore A in the upper left corner of these notecards identifies that source, and (iv) indicates the page number.

A. **Direct quotation (verbatim).** Be accurate; copy from the printed page exactly. Do not change the punctuation or the spelling; if there is an error, copy it and add *sic* in brackets. Enclose within double quotation marks all that you copy.

If there are double quotation marks within the passage, they will become single marks within your double ones. See card A.

A

A	
(iv)	"It seemed obvious to me that Arthur Miller's concept, expressed in 'Tragedy and the Common Man,' which recognizes the need for tragedy to be concerned with 'the heart and spirit of the average man,' provided enough reason to the contrary to permit me to substantiate an argument for the existence of tragedy in the twentieth century."

A

Either omit "to the contrary"
and use ellipsis marks or else
add in brackets an explanation
so that later you will know what
was meant by the phrase "the
contrary."

B. **Direct quotation of all or part of a passage with allowable changes:**

1. Ellipsis (the omission of a word or passage indicated
   by three periods with a space before and
   after and between each period). See card B.

B

A

(iv) "Two of the novels of William Faulkner, The
Sound and the Fury and Light in August,
have provided . . . a tremendous stimulus
for thought."

B

The words omitted contained a
pronoun referring to the author
and a phrase referring to another idea on the page. Neither
was needed to make this statement.

2. Brackets (used to enclose material you add within the quotation or to indicate a change in the form of some word). See card B2.

B2

A

(iv)   "Knowing the characteristics of classical tragedy, I could not read these novels (The Sound and the Fury, Light in August) without an awareness of their basic similarity to the tragic form in spite of the idea that Joseph Wood Krutch expresses to the contrary . . . concerning the inability of modern writers to create tragedy because of their lack of tragic faith."

The titles were in another sentence, but need to be inserted here if you are to know which novels *these* refers to. They could be abbreviated S.F. and L.A. if you used them often on other cards.

3. Certain limited changes without brackets:

a. Capitals may be made lower case (or vice versa) if such a change will enable you to use the quotation as part of your own sentence. Lower case letters may be capitalized if you want to begin a sentence in the middle of a sentence from your source. See card B3.

B3

A

ⓘⓥ   "The inability of modern writers to create
tragedy" is a concern of Joseph Wood Krutch,
but "two of the novels of William Faulkner"
are considered to be tragedy by some critics.

B3
The was not capitalized, but
two was.

b. A final (or internal) punctuation mark within a
quoted passage may be altered or omitted for the
same reason. Or you may add a period if you
terminate a quotation before the end of the sentence. See card B4.

B4

A

ⓘⓥ   "Arthur Miller . . . recognizes the need
for tragedy to be concerned with 'the heart
and spirit of the average man.'"

B4
There was a comma after *man*.

c. Tense may be altered to make the material fit the context of your own paper. See card B5.

B5

A

(iv)   "The best prose of William Faulkner qualifies him as a modern tragedian" and with it Hoffman "substantiates (her) argument for the existence of tragedy in the twentieth century."

B5

Qualifies was past tense; *substantiates* was an infinitive, and *her* was *my.*

d. Italics in the original will be indicated by underlining. If for emphasis you want to italicize words
not italicized in the original, so indicate after the
quotation by parentheses in which you say (Italics
mine). See card B6.

B6

A

(iv)   A close reading of the novels of
Faulkner will make obvious "their basic
similarity to the tragic form" of Greek
plays. In fact, "the best prose of
William Faulkner qualifies him as a
modern tragedian" and makes clear "the
existence of tragedy in the twentieth
century." (Italics mine.)

B6

The three quoted passages were
in different sentences and not in
this order; the past tense verb
(*qualified*) was changed to present tense so it would go with the
present tense verb *makes*.

NOTE: These three short quoted passages would be
documented in a single footnote.

C. Précis. This is a careful re-write in your own words,
usually about one-third the length of the original. In
writing a précis, you are actually composing part of
your paper. It is important to maintain the style, the
point of view, and the tone of the original without
using exact words or phrases from your source. See
card C.

C

A

(iv) William Faulkner's novels stimulate our
thinking. The qualities of traditional
tragedy are to be found in his best novels.
Krutch believes that today's writers cannot write tragedy because they lack faith
in the basic nobility of man, but A. Miller
believes that tragedy is concerned with
the life and soul of ordinary people.
Taking our cue from Miller and using
Faulkner's finest work, we can see that F.
is a twentieth century tragedian.

C

A capital **P** in parentheses will
remind you later that the words
are your own; you would then
footnote the idea but would not
put quotation marks around it.
Do the same for paraphrases.

D. Summary. This kind of note states in your own words
and/or condenses the basic ideas of a long passage,
chapter, or even whole book. See card D.

D

> **A**
>
> ⓘⓥ   F. writes trag. Krutch says that
>   trag. is not possible today, but
>   Miller says it is.

E. Outline. This kind of note reduces to organized form
the basic information in a paragraph, page, or chapter. See card E.

E

> **A**
>
> ⓘⓥ   F. = tragedian
>
>   A. characteristics of classical tragedy
>   B.   "   "   modern   "   (Miller)

F. Paraphrase. Use this with caution, for it is easy to be
careless and end up being a plagiarist. You will avoid
this danger if you read the passage well, close the book,
and then write your paraphrase from memory. The
paraphrase (see card F) is good to use

1. when you need to simplify some pedantic or esoteric
   passage;
2. when you re-phrase or clarify another's definition
   or explanation;
3. when you put the lines of a poem into your own
   words.

F

A

(iv) The fiction of F. is very stimulating. Many
of the characteristics of classical tragedy
can be found in his novels. In "The Tragic
Fallacy," J. W. Krutch says that modern writers
cannot write tragedy because they do not have
faith in man's nobility, a faith essential to
tragedy. A. Miller believes that trag. should
deal with the soul and life of the common man
and that trag. is therefore possible today.
To some, Faulkner's best work shows that he
does write tragedy.

(P)

NOTE: Indicate the beginning of any paraphrase by
informally mentioning the author or the
work or both as with Krutch and Miller
above.

G. Combination note. While you are making your notes,
you will occasionally find it advisable to weave a quotation into a sentence of your own to remind you of
how you intended to use the material or to enable you
to use the card intact in your rough draft. The only
danger lies in possible carelessness: be sure to make
clear (even exaggerated) quotation marks around the
quoted part of the sentence to distinguish it from your
own words. See card G.

G

A

(iv)   A close reading of the novels of Faulkner
will make obvious "their basic similarity
to the tragic form" of Greek plays. In
fact, Faulkner's writing makes clear "the
existence of tragedy in the twentieth
century."

H. Quotation taken from a footnote. It is important to
indicate the source quoted in the footnote of the
author you are reading; then any error in the quotation or publication data will be his, not yours. His
source will not be included in your bibliography. See
card H.

H

A

(iv)   Hoffman quotes Arthur Miller, "Tragedy and
the Common Man," The New York Times,
February 27, 1949, II, 3, as saying that
"tragedy implies more optimism in its
author than does comedy."

I. Quotation of a quote. Use this rarely. If a quotation
is valuable enough to quote, you should try to see the
original from which the quote was taken. However,
since some material used by other writers might be

difficult for you to obtain, this kind of note might be necessary. The source quoted by the author you read will not be included in your bibliography. See card I.

I

A	
(iv)	"Tragedy (is) concerned with 'the heart and spirit of the average man'" and is therefore universal in its appeal.

NOTE: If you used this sentence in your paper, your footnote would cite Hoffman as your source, not Miller. The identification at the top of the card already indicates that Hoffman is your source, but you might make a note of the fact that she was quoting Miller. Then add information about his article; you may be able to locate it for yourself.

J. **Critical.** You may wish to make an evaluation of the material you are reading or to write down your own ideas about it. This kind of note reminds you of judgments made during your reading. See card J.

J

A

(iv)   Hoffman dismisses Krutch too summarily.

K. Synopsis or condensation. This is a summary of narrative material (*i.e.*, a motion picture, a novel, a play, a narrative poem, etc.). No illustration card is given.

NOTE: Every completed notecard (see Steps 6 and 7) should have six items on it:

1. source symbol
2. page number in a circle
3. the note itself
4. quotation marks around verbatim quotes OR the letter *p* to indicate your personal wording or paraphrase
5. the label (slug) or an outline symbol
6. on the back, information about where you discovered that this source exists AND a note to yourself about how or why you plan to use it.
   (If your instructor prefers, put this information on the back of the bibliography card instead.)

   Remember these rules for punctuating with quotation marks: all commas and periods go *inside* the closing quotation marks; all other punctuation goes inside *only* when it is a part of the quoted matter; all semicolons go outside the closing marks.

LABEL NOTECARDS AND
REVISE WORKING OUTLINE

After you have taken about half of your notes, you will observe that they can be categorized under several general headings. Often these headings coincide with the various units of your preliminary outline; on the other hand, they often suggest topics which need to be added to your outline. Remember, as you read, that you will not only be revising your preliminary outline, but you should also be re-evaluating and re-formulating your thesis statement in the light of your increased knowledge and accumulated information.

The items of your preliminary outline will provide the labels or slugs which you will write in pencil on the top lines of your notecards; pencil is better than ink here because you may want to change your label if you find later that a particular note could be used better under another heading. Some material cannot be categorized easily; leave these notecards to be labeled later. Some notes will be particularly good as part of an introduction or a conclusion; use "intro." or "concl." as the slugs for these. Some notes will obviously not belong at all; mark these with an X and put them aside for the time being.

As you come closer to finishing your research, you will find that your notecards fall into four or five general categories, and these might turn out to be quite different from your original points for the temporary outline. You should now study your notecards and group them under general categories. Simply separate your cards into stacks, according to the ideas on them. This may take considerable time, but it is time well spent for here you will determine the organization of your entire paper.

If, for example, you were doing a paper on Faulkner as a writer of tragedy similar to that of Euripides, you might see that your cards can be divided into those characteristics of tragedy which are manifested in Euripides (such as his humanistic approach to tragedy), his psychological approach to tragedy, his thematic interest in "life as it ought to be" instead of "life as it is," and so forth. These classifications could then become the Roman numerals for your outline. Then you would further divide your cards into several sub-point labels, and one notecard might be labeled thus:

C   Eur: psych. app.--illus. in Medea

(24)   Eur. is interested in the heart and
        soul of his characters. He wants to know
        why they react as they do; what their
        psych. motiv. is. Why, for ex., did Medea
        kill her children?

NOTE: This card would go with IB on the outline, p. 97.

If, on the other hand, you were doing your research on the subject of smog control, you might find that your notecards will fall into such categories as causes of the smog problem, manifestations of the smog problem, effects of smog on various aspects of the environment, solutions to the problem of smog control. These general classifications would then supply the Roman numerals for your outline.

You may find other possibilities for different classifications by studying the following as they might relate to your subject:

problem—cause—effect—solution

social causes—political causes—economic causes— psychological causes

the various effects (or solutions or manifestations) of some problem

different kinds of irony or values or attitudes

different (or similar) characteristics of something or someone

different ways of evaluating your topic

different advantages (or disadvantages) of a particular method, machine, approach, or process

After you have found a way to divide your notecards into separate larger classifications, mark with a Roman numeral I all the cards in the classification you think you will discuss first in your paper; use a II for those you will discuss in the second part, and so on. Then take all the ones you have marked with numeral I and, considering them as material for a separate essay, determine into what categories you can further divide those ideas. For example, you might find that the pile of cards marked I, because they all deal with the causes of the smog problem (#2 in the list above), contain some that deal with problems related to industry, others deal with problems related to transportation, others with problems related to private homes. These would be divided into IA, IB, and IC. Then you would consider each of these sections separately. You might decide that those cards marked IA or IB do not need further division, but that those marked IC need to be divided into such categories as road transportation and air transportation, and you would mark the cards appropriately IC 1 and IC 2.

Remember in your outlining that you can never have a I without at least a II, nor an A without at least a B, nor a 1 without at least a 2, since logically nothing can be divided into fewer than two parts (not even apples). And your outline actually represents a division of ideas for the purpose of analyzing a subject in an organized fashion. At first, then, your notecards might have a label or slug like the example above; but once your outline is really set, you can save time by simply using the outline number instead.

Now you are ready to write the outline in its final form, taking care to word the items so that all Roman numerals (subdivisions of your thesis) are worded to be parallel in logic and in grammar; all the letter entries (A, B, C) are stated as parallel subdivisions of the Roman numeral under which they appear; and all the numbered entries (1, 2, 3) are logically and grammatically parallel subdivisions of the statement made in the letter under which they appear.

Before you can decide that you have finished your notetaking, you should examine your notecards to determine if you have adequate material for all the areas that are important to your thesis or a particular part of its proof. This evaluation will direct any subsequent notetaking to those specific topics for which you need more information, and you will then take only those notes which you know you will use. If you do take more notes on some new material that necessitates the inclusion of a new point, be sure to change your outline to include it.

WRITE THE FIRST DRAFT

Although you will never have the feeling that you have finished your notetaking to your satisfaction and you will never lose the feeling that you could do a much better job if you could examine "just one more source," the time for writing the first draft inevitably comes.

1. Check your thesis; be sure that it states as specifically as possible in a simple declarative sentence exactly what the material you have gathered adds up to.

2. Check your outline; be sure that each sub-topic is directly relevant to the more general topic above it and, finally, that each major topic is directly relevant to the thesis. Make each item parallel to every other item both logically and grammatically. (That is, in a sentence outline, which is definitely preferable to a topic outline, be sure that each item is stated in a full sentence; in a topic outline, be sure that all items are stated in parallel parts of speech which are also parallel logically.) Check to see that no item overlaps another. Remember that no item can be divided into just one part: every I must have a II, every A must have a B, every 1 must have a 2, and so forth. Check to see that you have arranged the items of your outline in logical order: order of space or time, order of importance, order of complexity, and so forth. REMEMBER: Just as it is better and more advantageous to detect the faults in a floor plan for a house on the blueprint than it is to find them in the finished building, so it is

easier and more advantageous to find the errors of your logic and organization in your outline than it is to find them in your finished paper.

3. Your outline should now be ready for you to write in its final form if you have followed the instructions in Step 6. If you have some notecards you cannot use (there are inevitably a few), do not destroy them; put them away, for you may be able to use them in writing some other paper in the future.

4. Do not begin by writing your introduction. Wait to write that when your paper is completed and you can see what you are introducing. Start now by putting on paper as quickly as possible the over-all information you wish to convey about your major points and their subdivisions. Save the fun of polishing your style till later; first you must capture your ideas on paper so you can think about them.

   Develop your first point first. Arrange the note-cards for your first Roman numeral to correspond with the order in that part of your outline and plunge right in as if you were writing a short essay with Roman numeral I as your thesis.

5. Write on one side of the paper only and skip a line between each line of your writing so that you can cross out poor or awkward phrases and add better wording without unnecessary recopying later when you revise. If you type your draft, triple space for the same reason.

6. If you use a direct quote in your paper, simply staple or clip the notecard on which it is written to the place where it belongs in your text. This will save time and avoid the possibility of inaccuracy as a result of re-copying.

It is very important to learn how to "weave" quoted or paraphrased material so that it becomes a part of your own text. Try not to use the colon to introduce any quotation unless it is long enough to block (i.e., one over three lines in length); otherwise, weave quotations into your own sentences so that a person hearing the paper read aloud would be unable to tell where a quote actually begins or ends. Make all quoted material sound like an integral part of your whole work; this means you must pay attention to point of view and tense. Not only does integrating the source material into your text add to the general unity and fluency of your writing; it also serves the even more important purpose of indicating relevance to the content of your paper. In other words, before using a quoted or paraphrased passage, think of why you are using it or of what purpose it serves in your paragraph; then weave it into your text by indicating some relevance which you clarify in your own wording. It will then be valuable to your proof of thesis, and its implications will be clear to your reader.

For example, in the following sentence from a discussion of Gerhart Hauptmann's play *The Weavers,* there is no doubt about the significance of the quotation used:

The formula for success, which according to Master Wiegand is "cunning, quickness, and ruthless determination" [p. 30], had to be exposed and challenged.

Poorly used, the quotation might be inserted without any indication of relevance to the purpose of the paper, which (as here) might be a study of the values questioned in the play. An example of the same quotation, ineptly used, might read thus:

> Master Wiegand said: "Cunning, quickness, and ruthless determination are necessary" [p. 30].

Your reader would naturally wonder, "Necessary for what?" You might profit at this point by studying pages 99-101 to see the variety of ways to incorporate quotations into your text. Note the punctuation also.

> NOTE: The physical presence of the notecards on the first draft will do more than save you time and eliminate the possibility of inaccurate copying; it will also

1. help you see if you are merely "stringing quotes" without enough of your own wording;

2. keep you from using and footnoting the same information or the same quoted passage twice;

3. help you check the way you introduce each quoted passage or phrase.

7. Even before you finish the first writing (rough draft), you may want to rearrange some material already written. If so, see the first two paragraphs under STEP 8; the directions there will facilitate your work if you decide to insert or change material as you write.

8. When you have taken information from a notecard, whether it is a directly quoted passage or not, stop where the passage ends and draw in the cut-off lines across your page. Be sure to do this at the exact point where the material

AA, ⑦⑦

calls for a footnote. Leave enough space so that you can fill in your full footnote later; right now, while your notecard is in your hand, simply put in the bibliography card identification letter (like AA above) and the page number (like ⑦⑦ above) from which the information came. It is helpful to write footnote information in a different color of ink. It is essential to copy this information exactly; it is the only way that you can be assured that your documentation is accurate.

Put a check in the corner of the notecard that you have used so that you will be sure not to use the same information again. If your cut-off lines come in the middle of the sentence, continue after the cut-off lines as if they were not there.

9. Repeat this process to develop each of your Roman numerals, considering each as a separate essay for the time being. Just as you could not expect to write five essays in one day, so you can not hope to develop more than one section of a long paper at a time.

10. Remember to revise your outline if you make any changes as you write your first draft. By the time you complete your first draft, your outline will be the blueprint of your actual paper.

11. Be sure to number the pages of your first draft; if you add pages to be inserted between pages already numbered, simply number the inserted pages also; for example, if they come after page 8, number the inserted pages 8A, 8B, and so on, but remember to re-number the inserted pages (and all subsequent pages) before typing your final copy.

REVISE THE TEXT;
WRITE INTRODUCTION
AND CONCLUSION

The best way to revise your work is to read your paper aloud after a waiting period. Avoid the necessity of re-copying your work by using scissors to cut out material which belongs elsewhere. Be sure to cut out any footnote that belongs with a passage you are moving. Simply scotch tape the whole insert where it belongs; you may need to cut that page in order to insert the interpolated material.

The advantage of keeping the footnote within cut-off lines immediately below the material it documents and the advantage of not numbering the footnotes until the paper is ready for typing are obvious here. You are free to move material around without recopying, without the chance of inaccurate documentation, and without having to re-number all of the succeeding footnotes. Your draft is supposed to look quite worked over, crossed out, and rearranged as a result of your revision.

1. Check to see that you have followed the basic rules for good English sentence structure and style.

2. Check to see that you have followed the principles of rhetoric in your sentence structure, paragraph development, and diction.

3. Check to see that you have smooth transitions (connections) from sentence to sentence, paragraph to para-

graph, and section to section. Check particularly to see that the quoted material is integrated into the text so that together with your writing it presents a unified piece of work. Check also the punctuation before and after the quoted material used as part of your own sentence; a good test is to ask yourself whether you would use a comma, a colon, or other punctuation if there were no quotation marks within that sentence. (See Card G, p. 60.) When you hear a well-prepared lecture, you are not aware that the lecturer has gathered his material from many different sources, some of which he is quoting directly and others of which he is paraphrasing. You should give the same impression to your reader. Often the addition of a few connecting words will result in smooth transitions.

4. Check to see that your finished paper sounds logically developed and that everything that you have included in your paper presents relevant, logical proof of your thesis.

5. Check to see that you have avoided the repetition of facts or ideas. A "padded" paper is boring and meaningless.

Write the introduction

Now that you know exactly what you are about to introduce, you can write an introductory section to your paper. You can use your introduction to do the following:

1. point out the timeliness or value of your research;
2. define an abstract or special term used in your thesis;
3. explain why you have taken this particular aspect of your topic;
4. inform your reader of the various aspects of your topic other than the one you have chosen;

5. give a pertinent anecdote which provides a direct means of leading into your topic;
6. summarize how you have approached your topic.

Whatever your approach, your introduction should be relevant; it should gain the immediate attention of your reader; and it should clarify your thesis in some way.

Write the conclusion

The conclusion of the research paper is the most valuable single part of it. All the material you have gathered means nothing to your reader until you present the conclusion you have reached as a result of your research. Re-state your thesis and show what the material you have presented adds up to. Analyze and evaluate your main points for your reader; also consider the ramifications and general implications of them to your conclusion. Actually, the conclusion is the only "original" contribution you offer in your paper. It manifests the value of your research as well as your understanding of the material which you have presented.

FILL IN FOOTNOTES ON DRAFT

Before you put your paper into its final copy form, you need to fill in the footnotes within the cut-off lines and write them as they will appear in your final paper. Normally, every paragraph except those which develop your own completely original ideas will have at least one footnote.

What to footnote

1. All important statements of fact and all opinions, whether directly quoted or paraphrased, and all paraphrases of those facts which are not common knowledge should be documented by a footnote reference to the exact page in the source where you found your information. If you are not quoting printed matter, your footnote should tell the reader where and how you found out the particular material you need to document.

2. Definitions which would interrupt the text but which might be helpful to the reader should be in a footnote.

3. Material which would detract from the focus of your paper but which would supply valuable and enriching information to the reader should be in a footnote, not in the text of your paper. This material may be in your own words or in words you quote from an authority. Also, the footnote may simply refer the reader to another source or sources where a fuller discussion may be found.

4. Cross-references may be suggested in a footnote. Often you want to show the existence of contradictory information or to refer your reader to additional sources.

5. Cross-references to other parts of your own paper may be made in footnotes.

What not to footnote

1. All well-known, generally accepted facts need not be footnoted unless you want to document someone's questioning of those facts.

2. Any material which comes from commonly recognized sources or quotations need not be footnoted; you may say that all men are created equal or that all the world's a stage or that the heavens declare the glory of God without referring in context or footnote to the Declaration of Independence, to Shakespeare, or to the Bible, respectively.

How to complete footnotes within cut-off lines

After the last revision work on the text of your rough draft, go through it once more and number the items to be footnoted. Put the number after the last word before the cut-off lines and above the line of writing. If you are documenting a direct quote, put the number after the closing quotation mark. Put the same number after the abbreviated symbol for the source already within the cut-off lines. Your footnote number will then be indented as it must be when you put the paper into final form. Number consecutively throughout your paper.

You will now use the completed bibliography card to complete your footnote. For every first-entry footnote (the first time you document information from a source) you will give the complete bibliographical information *plus* the exact page number which you have already entered in the cut-off lines. For all succeeding footnotes referring to that source, use the second-entry form.

Indent the first line of each footnote as for a paragraph and bring each succeeding line of the same footnote back to the margin.

Procedure for writing footnotes

1. Take out the bibliography card indicated by the letter or symbol already entered in the cut-off lines.

2. Write your footnote as you would a sentence; do not separate into lines as you did on the bibliography card.

3. Write the number of the footnote in either of two ways, but be consistent:

   a. above the line as it must be in the text, or
   b. on the same line as the footnote will be.

   For the former, use no period after the number; for the latter, be sure to use a period and two spaces before beginning your footnote. Check to see that the number in the text matches the number given for the footnote. Remember that footnotes are numbered consecutively throughout the paper; there will be only one footnote numbered 1 in any short paper (fewer than fifty typewritten pages) or for each chapter in a long paper.

4. Indent the footnote number and first line as for a paragraph; bring the second and each succeeding line of the same note back to the margin of the text.

5. Fill in all information from the bibliography card exactly as it is written with these exceptions:

   a. write the author's name in regular order (not reversed) followed by a comma, not a period;

b. omit the period after the name of a book; put a comma instead of a period after the name of an article;

c. enclose within parentheses the publication facts for a book (city, publisher, date), omitting the period after the date; put a comma after the parentheses.

6. Copy exactly the page number already after the symbol at the beginning of the cut-off lines; unless a volume number is given, put the abbreviation for *page* before the page number. If a pamphlet or booklet has no page number, supply a page number in brackets or write these words after the comma: no page.

7. Put a period at the end of the footnote.

8. Check the page number which you had entered in the cut-off lines after the symbol for the source to be sure it matches the page number in the footnote; cross out both symbol and page number, leaving only the completed footnote form within the cut-off lines.

9. Before you put your bibliography card away, put a check mark by the identifying letter or symbol on it (the one you used on notecards) to show that you have used this source once for a first-entry footnote.

10. All future references to this source or to any other source already documented in full will be in second-entry footnote form.

How to write footnotes on the final copy

1. Decide where you are going to put your footnotes; there are three acceptable places:

a. at the bottom of the same page on which the footnote number occurs in the text; for this place, triple space after the last line of text and then make a line by striking the underline key fifteen times; then double space before writing the footnote number, then give the typewriter carriage half a turn downward before writing the footnote. Remember to indent the first line of each footnote five spaces as if for a paragraph; bring the rest of the footnote back to the margin. Single space each entry; double space between each footnote entry.

b. on a separate page at the end of a short paper or at the end of each chapter for a long paper; for this page, center and type the title in capitals (FOOT-NOTES) with no underlining; put the page number in the center at the bottom of the page. If there is more than one page, put no heading or title on the next page, but continue to number in the upper right-hand corner to match the pagination on other pages.

c. in the text itself; it is becoming increasingly popular for instructors to suggest that relatively short papers be documented within the text itself in order to avoid numerous footnotes at the bottom of the page or at the end of the paper on a separate page. This in-text documentation is especially desirable when a student uses only one source or only a few sources about his subject. To use in-text documentation, give the first-entry footnote in full at the bottom of the page as explained in *a* above or within the text itself as explained on pages 89–90; then insert in brackets each succeeding footnote for any quote or paraphrase from that source, placing the brackets directly after it (see examples below). Generally, if the footnote contains a definition or explanation, or if it is more than three-fourths of a line in length, you should use the regular footnote form at the bottom of the page or at the end of your paper.

Examples of In-Text Documentation:

If you were doing a critical analysis of a single text, such as Faulkner's *The Sound and the Fury*, you would give a formal first-entry footnote after your first reference to the book. You might even add a sentence after that footnote and as a part of it, stating that all future references to this text are from the same edition. Then the second time you document from the book, your text would look like this:

> Mrs. Compson looks upon Benjy as "a judgment" [p. 25], and she changes his name, not wanting an idiot child to bear the name of her brother because she is "too proud" [p. 89].

NOTE: The punctuation comes after the bracket closes.

If you are using two texts by the same author, you would give the first-entry footnotes in full for each book; for all later quotations you would give the name of the work in brackets so that your reader would know to which of the two sources your documentation refers. For example: [*The Sound and the Fury*, p. 62] or [Light in August, p. 104].

If you are using several texts all by different authors, you would give the first-entry footnotes in full as in both examples above and then put the author's name and the page in brackets after the reference, thus:

[Miller, p. 240] or [Shaw, p. 69].

2. Copy the footnote exactly as you have written it within the cut-off lines.

3. Single space the lines within each footnote entry and double space between entries.

Forms for first-entry footnotes from a book

NOTE: Some writers do not include in footnotes all of the publication data if a bibliography is given at the end of the paper; however, many colleges do require the following full form as well as a bibliography.

1. one author
[1] Richard B. Sewall, *The Vision of Tragedy* (New Haven: Yale University Press, 1959), p. 12.

2. a chapter or a section of a book
[2] Alfred Kazin, "Liberals and New Humanists," *On Native Grounds* (Garden City, New York: Doubleday & Company, Inc., 1956), pp. 197-238.

3. two authors
[3] Harry Modean Campbell and Ruel E. Foster, *William Faulkner: A Critical Appraisal* (Norman: University of Oklahoma Press, 1951), p. 36.

4. more than two authors
[4] Joseph M. Bachelor and others, *Current Thinking and Writing*, 3rd series (New York: Appleton-Century-Crofts, Inc., 1956), p. vii.

5. **an editor in addition to an author** (collected works of one author with an editor)

[5] William Wordsworth, *The Prelude or Growth of a Poet's Mind,* Ernest de Selincourt, ed. (New York: Oxford University Press, 1947), p. 16.

6. **an editor but no author**

[6] Frederick L. Gwynn and Joseph L. Blotner, eds., *Faulkner in the University* (Charlottesville: University of Virginia Press, 1959), p. 21.

7. **an author, a translator, and an editor**

[7] Euripides, *Bacchae,* trans. Henry Birkhead, *Ten Greek Plays in Contemporary Translations,* L. R. Lind, ed. (Boston: Houghton Mifflin Co., 1957), p. 325.

> NOTE: If you have a book without one of these, the form is the same; simply omit the one or two names missing.

8. **an editor, but no author** (not an anthology)

[8] *Great Dialogues of Plato,* trans. W. H. D. Rouse. Eric H. Warmington and Philip G. Rouse, eds. (New York: The New American Library of World Literature, Inc., 1956), pp. 393-94.

9. **a book in a series edited by one other than the author**

[9] Vincent H. Malstrom and Ruth M. Malstrom, *Norway* in the "Life in Europe" series, Raymond E. Fideler and others, ed. (Grand Rapids, Michigan: Fideler Company, 1955), pp. 21-22.

10. **one volume with a separate title in a multi-volume set**

[10] Vernon Louis Parrington, *The Romantic Revolu-*

tion in America, 1800-1860 (Vol. II of *Main Currents in American Thought,* 3 vols.; New York: Harcourt, Brace and Company, 1927-30), 65.

11. a book or article quoted in a source you read (secondary source citation)

[11] Joseph Wood Krutch, "The Tragic Fallacy," *The Modern Temper: A Study and a Confession* (New York: Harcourt, Brace and Co., 1956), pp. 79-97, quoted by Roberta G. Hoffman, "Tragedy: from Athens to Yoknapatawpha" (unpublished Master's thesis, Department of English, Columbia University, 1961), p. iv.

12. one volume in a multi-volume set (all volumes with the same title)

[12] Euripides, *Orestes,* trans. E. P. Coleridge (Vol. II of *The Complete Greek Drama,* Whitney J. Oates and Eugene O'Neill Jr, eds., 2 vols.; New York: Random House, 1938), 111-70.

Forms for first-entry footnotes from sources contained in a larger work

13. an encyclopedia article

[13] George G. A. Murray, "Greek Drama: Origins," *Encyclopaedia Britannica* (1958), VII, 578.

   NOTE: If the article is unsigned, start with the name of the article.

14. a critical comment in a reprint

[14] Andrew Wright, "Afterword," in Joyce Cary, *The Horse's Mouth* (London, 1944; rpt. New York: Perennial Library ed.—Harper & Row, 1965), p. 351.

15. a newspaper article or an editorial, signed

[15] Arthur Miller, "Tragedy and the Common Man," *The New York Times,* February 27, 1949, II, 1, 3.

> NOTE: The first footnote for a work with a long title may indicate the shortened title you intend to use in subsequent footnotes. After the period, indicate how you will identify the work:
> Cited hereafter as Miller, "Tragedy."

16. an essay (or other article) **written by one person in an anthology edited by another**

[16] George Orwell, "Politics and the English Language," *The Pursuit of Learning,* Nathan Comfort Starr, ed. (New York: Harcourt, Brace and Company, 1956), p. 46.

17. a part of a book with its own author in a book or series edited by others

[17] William Arrowsmith, "Introduction to *Hecuba,*" *Euripides* (Vol. III of *The Complete Greek Tragedies,* David Grene and Richmond Lattimore, eds.; Chicago: The University of Chicago Press, 1959), p. 490.

> NOTE: The volume number and the name of the series are enclosed in parentheses with the facts of publication to indicate that *Euripides* is the title of Volume III only.

18. an article with no author

[18] "10 Amazing Years: 1947-1957," *U. S. News & World Report,* December 27, 1957, p. 42.

19. a letter to the editor

[19] Norma Liss, "Pear Trees and the Artist," in "Letters to the Editor," *Saturday Review of Literature,* August 2, 1952, p. 25.

20. a well-known literary work which can be identified by chapter and verse or by book or scene and act plus lines

[20] John Milton, *Paradise Lost,* Book I, ll. 254-55.

21. a verse in the Bible

[21] I Corinthians 13:12 (R.S.V.).

22. essay in a casebook

[22] David Stevenson, "J. D. Salinger: The Mirror of Crisis," *Nation,* March 9, 1957, in *If You Really Want to Know: a CATCHER Casebook,* Malcolm M. Marsden, ed. (Chicago: Scott, Foresman and Company, 1963), p. 215.

23. record jacket information

[23] Record jacket information, *The Bitter and the Sweet,* Peter Seeger (Columbia Records, 1962. CS 8716).

24. a lecture on a record or tape

[24] Thomas Scherman, "Musical Program Notes," Beethoven's *Symphony No. 5 in C Minor* (Vanguard, MARS 3005).

25. movie

[25] William Shakespeare, Romeo and Juliet. Franco Zeffirelli, director-producer. Paramount, 1968.

26. television program

[26] Room 222 (ABC series): "Once Upon a Time There Was Air You Couldn't See." KABC (TV Channel 7), Los Angeles, January 28, 1970.

27. radio program

[27] Jason Joe Fuller, "Forecast for the Future," Radio broadcast, KTAM, Phoenix, January 30, 1970.

28. a pamphet included with a record

[28] Richard Kostelanetz and the Editors of Time-Life Records, "A Listener's Guide to the Recordings," *The Music of Today* in "The Story of Great Music" series (New York: Time Incorporated, 1967), Time-Life Records, STL145.

Abbreviated forms for second-entry footnotes

When you take out a bibliography card and see the check which indicates that you already have a first-entry footnote for that source, use the appropriate second-entry form for that and all subsequent footnotes referring to that source. The abbreviated, second-entry forms for footnotes have traditionally been given in Latin terms, but current usage seems to indicate the eventual elimination of all Latin from footnotes.

Some scholars have already eliminated all Latin terms except *ibid. Vide* has already been replaced by "see" which is shorter and requires no underlining; *op. cit.* and *loc. cit.* are considered obsolete and are no longer required in many schools. However, since they are still frequently found in older reference materials, you need to know what they signify and you will find an explanation below.

1. **for a footnote which is identical in all respects to the last footnote referring to any source:**

    There may be intervening footnotes (giving a definition, an explanation, or a cross-reference) between *ibid.* and the source to which it refers, so long as no other source is mentioned in them.

    The previous source need not be mentioned on the same page as *ibid.*

    [1] *Ibid.*

    Although *ibid.* may be the first footnote to appear on a page, it obviously could never be the first footnote of a paper.

2. **for a footnote identical in all respects except page number to the last footnote referring to any source (see note above):**

[2] *Ibid.,* p. 16.	With or without a page number, *ibid.* is no longer used by many scholars; the last name of the author and the page number are often used instead. See the footnotes on pages 103-104 listed after the sample paper.

3. **for a footnote referring to a source after which another source intervenes (there are two acceptable forms):**

[3] Miller, p. 3.	This form will adequately identify any source already cited in full except when there are two sources by the same author or two authors with the same last name. See 4 and 5 below.

[3] Miller, *op. cit.,* p. 3.

Although you may not be required to use this form, you will still find it in some older writings and will need to know what it means.

4. **for a footnote referring to a source if you have used two or more sources by the same author:**

[4] Milton, *Paradise Lost,* Book I, 1. 254.

To distinguish which of his works you are quoting, give the author's last name, the full title of the source or a shortened form of it, and the page number.

[4] Miller, "Tragedy . . . ," p. 3.

5. **for a footnote to distinguish between two or more authors with the same last name:**

   5 John A. Miller, pp. 26-28.

   > This would be enough if you have previously cited only one work by this author.

   5 John A. Miller, *Greek Tragedy,* pp. 26-28.

   > If you have previously cited two or more sources by this author, give also the title or a shortened form of it to show which source you are now citing.

6. **for a footnote referring to the same page as the last citation from a source, after which another source has intervened:**

   6 Miller, p. 3.

   > Use this preferred form if you have previously quoted from only one source by Miller.

   6 Miller, "Tragedy . . . ," p. 3.

   > After the author's name, give the title or a shortened form of it if you have previously quoted two sources by Miller.

7. **for a footnote referring to a source without an author:**

   7 "10 Amazing Years . . . ," p. 42.

   7 *Time, Talent, and Teachers,* [p. 3].

   > If a page has no number, supply one and put it in square brackets.

8. **for a second-entry footnote referring to an encyclopedia article:**

   8 Murray, "Greek Drama . . . ," p. 578.

   or, if it is unsigned,

   8 "Greek Tragedy," p. 1063.

9. for an incomplete second-entry footnote:

[9] P. 65.

> Use this form only if the author and source are already clear in the passage of the text numbered 29. Because it begins the footnote, P is capitalized.

[9] *The Vision of Tragedy,* p. 16.

> Use this form if you have named the author in the text and have also previously identified his work in a first-entry footnote.

NOTE: Although it is more helpful to your reader to see the full second-entry footnote, any information which is given in the text *may* correctly be omitted from the footnote. For example, if you name the author and/or the name of his work in your text, you may omit that information from your footnote and supply only what is needed to identify your exact source accurately. Therefore the above forms are sometimes used for second-entry footnotes.

Form for in-text documentation

When it is expedient to document within the text itself (*e.g.,* when there will be only one or two references in a short paper), you must still give complete bibliographical information. This may be given in an informal way within your own sentence:

> On page 3 of his *Story and Structure* published in New York in 1959 by Harcourt, Brace and Company, Inc., Laurence Perrine says that "fiction may be classified into two broad categories: literature of escape and literature of interpretation."

Or it may be given in this formal way or some variation of it:

Roberta Hoffman ("Tragedy: from Athens to Yoknapatawpha," unpublished Master's thesis, Department of English, Columbia University, 1961, p. iv)
is "convinced that the best prose of William Faulkner qualified him as a modern tragedian."
(See Also pp. 79–80)

Forms for special problems in footnotes

The following examples show several technicalities involved in using footnotes described in 3 under WHAT TO
FOOTNOTE (see pp. 75-76).

1. One is reminded here of Huxley's statement when
Mr. Propter says, "Because potential evil is *in* time; potential good isn't." Aldous Huxley, *After Many a Summer
Dies the Swan* (New York: Avon Publishing Co., Inc.,
1939), p. 122.
   "Actualized good . . . lies in timelessness." See *ibid.*,
p. 124.
   Ryan, p. 42, bases her parallel study of *The Sound
and the Fury* and Macbeth's speech from which the title
was taken on the fact that Quentin is the embodiment
of life as Macbeth sees it—empty, meaningless, and futile.
She explains that the dominant note is the despair at the
evil within and without, against which every tragic hero
struggles and which overwhelms Quentin.

2. The French poet, Pierre Emmanuel, "Faulkner
and the Sense of Sin," *The Harvard Advocate,* CXXXV
(November, 1951), 20, in a discussion of Faulkner's concept of time makes the statement that real time has nothing
to do with past, present, and future; "it is a simultaneous
though unconscious present. Something like God's eye."

3. Gwynn and Blotner, p. 17, quote Faulkner as
saying that there are "too many Quentins in the South who
are too sensitive to face its reality."

Many of Faulkner's critics have compared Quentin's ineffectuality to Hamlet's. Howe, *William Faulkner: A Critical Study, passim,* shows the parallel in detail. Cleanth Brooks, "Primitivism in *The Sound and the Fury,*" *English Institute Essays—1952,* Alan S. Downer, ed. (New York: Columbia University Press, 1953), pp. 5-28, also suggests this parallel. A parallel of Quentin's Southern heritage with Hamlet's father has also been suggested. All parallels are based, of course, on Quentin's inability to act.

PUT THE PAPER IN FINAL FORM

1. Format

If possible, a research paper should be typewritten on regular (never thin) paper and double-spaced except for blocked quotations, footnotes, and bibliography; otherwise, it should be written in blue or black ink as neatly and legibly as possible. Leave good margins on all four sides of the paper, allowing sufficient extra room on the left side for binding. The finished paper should be fastened and bound in a folder with the title, your name, the course, and the date on the outside.

2. Title page

Include a title page on which you state the title of the paper, your name, the course (and section number, if any) for which the paper was written, the name of the institution (often considered optional), and the date the paper is submitted.

3. Preface

The dedication or the preface page, if there is one, is inserted after the title page; it is not numbered. The title of the page, DEDICATION or PREFACE, is centered and typed with capital letters.

4. Outline

The outline page serves as a table of contents, although it is not necessary to show page numbers for the short paper. The title of the page, OUTLINE, is centered and typed in capital letters. The page is numbered, and since the first page of your outline is a title page, the number is centered at the bottom of the page and is given in Roman numerals (lower case) because nothing is numbered in Arabic numerals until the first page of the text.

After the title, OUTLINE, skip two spaces and state the thesis sentence (after the word THESIS:). Follow that statement with the outline proper.

5. First page of text

The title of your paper is centered on the first (and no other) page of the text and typed in capital letters.

6. Footnotes

The footnotes will be written exactly as you have filled them in on the rough draft of your paper. For detailed information concerning footnote forms on the final copy, see STEP 9, the section entitled HOW TO WRITE FOOT-NOTES ON THE FINAL COPY, pages 78 to 91. All footnotes should be completed on the page where they begin.

NOTE: There may be a rare occasion when you need to continue a footnote onto the following page. If so, it will continue as a sentence (without interruption) and will go immediately after the line separating text from footnotes or onto the next (untitled) page if you are placing footnotes at the end of your paper.

7. Pagination

Every page which is a title page (*i.e.,* the first page of the outline, of the footnotes, and of the bibliography; the dedication page; the preface; and so forth) is numbered at the bottom center of that title page. The number is written usually without punctuation. All other pages of the paper are numbered in the upper right-hand corner of the page; the number is written alone or followed by a period. The pages are numbered consecutively from the first page of the theme to the last page of the bibliography.

8. Quotations

Short quotations: Quoted short passages and/or sentences are woven into the text of your paragraph and should blend smoothly with your own style and the tense you are using. In the sample research paper on pages 96-106 you will see many examples of quotations (and paraphrases) woven into the text and made meaningful by the context in which they appear. Notice that before and after each quoted passage the punctuation is determined by what is needed to make the passage fit smoothly into the sentence. In other words, the test for punctuating before or after a quoted passage is this: Would you need a mark of punctuation at that point in your sentence if there were no quotation marks?

Longer (blocked) quotations: Sometimes, as in the passages numbered 13 and 21 in the sample paper, a quoted passage is too long to "weave" into your own sentence; it is an entity in itself and must be set off from the paragraph in which it appears. In fact, any directly quoted material which is longer than three lines must be blocked and single-spaced.

To set off a blocked passage: Double space before the quote; indent seven spaces for each regular line. Indent twelve spaces if the quotation itself begins with a new paragraph and seven spaces for each succeeding, single-spaced line. Stop seven spaces before the right-hand margin begins. Single space each line of the quoted passage, and then double space before the text of your paper continues. If the quoted and blocked passage is longer than one paragraph, double space between paragraphs within the same blocked passage. Do not use quotation marks at the beginning or end since the single spacing is a substitute for them.

However, you would use double or single quotation marks even in a blocked passage to enclose any material which is in double or single quotation marks in the source you are citing. In other words, a blocked quoted passage looks exactly as it did in the source you used.

Footnote number: The footnote number is put above the line and after the closing quotation mark or after the last word in a blocked passage.

9. Bibliography

The final bibliography is always the last section of a research paper. See STEP 4 for final bibliography forms.

10. Final Step

Proofread your paper carefully for typographical errors and use black ink to fill in brackets if needed.

A sample research paper

NOTE: Since it is neither expedient nor necessary to reproduce an entire paper for the sake of illustrating the techniques explained in this manual, the pages that follow contain a full sentence outline and only that part of the paper which expands the thesis. (Normally, the first part of any research paper, the introduction, usually develops the thesis and clarifies the point of view from which the writer has limited his paper.) Also included is a bibliography listing only the sources used in this introductory section of the longer paper by Hoffman, from which this section is taken.

TRAGEDY:

FROM ATHENS TO YOKNAPATAWPHA

by

Roberta M. Hoffman

English 250, Section 9

Columbia University

May 12, 1971

OUTLINE

Thesis: The best works of William Faulkner show that he
          has a tragic vision akin to that of Euripides and
          that he can be considered a tragedian in the
          classical sense.

    I. A study of Euripides reveals his particular
        interpretation of classical tragedy.

        A. His work shows Euripides' interest
            in humanism.

        B. His approach was a psychological one.

        C. His themes evolved from his question-
            ing of certain aspects of his
            contemporary society.

            1. He questioned the religious and
                philosophical concepts of his time.

            2. He questioned the conventions of
                his time.

   II. A study of Faulkner reveals that his tragic
        vision was similar to that of Euripides.

        A. Faulkner's best work shows an interest
            in humanism similar to that of
            Euripides.

        B. Faulkner's psychological approach to
            his characters was similar to that of
            Euripides.

        C. Faulkner's themes reveal his question-
            ing of certain aspects of twentieth-
            century society.

            1. He questioned the religious and
                philosophical concepts of his
                time.

            2. He questioned the conventions of
                twentieth century society.

iii

TRAGEDY:

FROM ATHENS TO YOKNAPATAWPHA

The perceptive scholar who has some awareness of the
tradition of classical tragedy cannot read the best works of
William Faulkner without concluding that he is one of the few
contemporary writers who may be truthfully called a "tragedian"
in the classical sense. Many Faulkner critics and scholars
have supported this view by making a study of one or another
of Faulkner's characters as tragic heroes according to the
Aristotelian formula, which includes the consequences of
harmartia and hubris, or by proving that a particular Faulknerian
novel, after providing the necessary inspiration of pity and
terror, affords the tragic experience of katharsis. Sewall,
for example, says that "although not alone in its generation,
the work of William Faulkner has gone farthest, I think, toward
restoring to fiction the full dimensions and the true dialectic
tension of tragedy."[1] Sewall further asserts that the testi-
mony of Faulkner's major works in view of their concern, their
method, and their purpose proves them to be basically tragic.[2]
Griffin also shows by his thesis that Faulkner falls into the
classic tradition because he objectifies his tragic conception
of man in the universe.[3] He feels that Faulkner is a great
tragedian because he revived "the tragic pattern,"[4] and he
very meticulously proves that many of Faulkner's characters are

1

2

symbols of this tragic pattern.[5] Mikules shows that in <u>Absalom,</u>
<u>Absalom!</u> and in <u>The Sound and the Fury</u> Faulkner approaches myth
as tragedy.[6] O'Donnell, pointing out that all of Faulkner's
work is a striving toward tragedy, reaches the conclusion that
much of his work achieves the highest form of that tradition.[7]

Leibowitz notes the general atmosphere of tragedy in
Faulkner's work: "prédispose l'artiste à une atmosphère
spirituelle specifique, qui est celle de la tragédie."[8] Cecil
Williams summarizes what many of the critics have observed when
he said that Faulkner "has the depth needed to provide the
Aristotelian catharsis; he has managed a Mississippian rein-
carnation of the Greek drama."[9]

After acknowledging the fact that Faulkner is a tragedian,
the scholar is understandably tempted to associate Faulkner
with one of the three great classical tragedians--Aeschylus,
Sophocles, or Euripides. Although one could certainly find
much from a study of any one of the three with which the tragedy of Faulkner could be identified,[10] it would appear that
the general focus and interest of Euripides provide the strong-
est basis for a comparative study. Possibly much of the reason
for this is also the reason that Euripides, more than Aeschylus
or Sophocles, "has perhaps more to say to the modern mind because his own so closely resembles it."[11] Hadas explains, for
example, that what Aeschylus and Sophocles "have to tell us is

profound and momentous, but it belongs in an abstract   3

realm not immediately relevant to ordinary experience. . . .

Euripides, by contrast, is nearer our own end of the

spectrum."[12]

In his study of Euripides, Lucas points out many of

the specific qualities and themes that make his work

particularly meaningful to the modern reader:

> the intense individualism, the bold ques-
> tioning of all orthodox tradition, . . . the
> realization that life is too complex for rules
> of thumb, that from all moral codes and catch-
> words and taboos there lies always the appeal
> to common sense and common humanity.[13]

Both Faulkner and Euripides are tragedians who follow

Aristotle's concept of tragedy fairly closely. They are

concerned with the imitation of life by means of language

and spectacle so as to arouse the tragic pleasure of pity

and fear, thus bringing about a <u>katharsis</u> of those emo-

tions.[14] However, their interpretations of Aristotle

closely approximate the modern theory of tragedy which

Arthur Miller articulated in his article, "Tragedy and the

Common Man."[15] No doubt it was because of the modernity

of the Euripidean interpretation of tragedy that Aristophanes

censured Euripides as he did. He disliked him because "he

is the spirit of the age personified, with its restlessness,

its skepticism, its sentimentalism, its unsparing question-

ing of old traditions, of religious usages and civic

loyalty."[16] Faulkner would also be guilty of this

accusation. What Aristophanes condemns, Arthur Miller's   4
interpretation of tragedy would accept. Miller says, for
example, that "no tragedy can . . . come about when
its author fears to question absolutely everything, when
he regards any institution, habit or custom as being either
everlasting, immutable or inevitable."[17] Both Faulkner
and Euripides would certainly agree. The work of both men
demonstrates "a revolutionary questioning of the stable
environment" that is terrifying,[18] and both see that "the
underlying struggle is that of the individual attempting
to gain his 'rightful' position in his society."[19] We find
in their work the balance between what is possible and
what is impossible that Miller considers essential to
tragedy as well as a humanistic belief in the perfectibility
of man.[20]

     When Faulkner was asked for his own interpretation of
Aristotle's "man of high place," he answered that Aristotle
meant a man of integrity.

> But tragedy, as Aristotle saw it, it's--I
> would say, is the same conception of tragedy
> that all writers have: it's man wishing to
> be braver than he is, in combat with his heart
> or with his fellows or with his environment,
> and how he fails, that the splendor, the
> courage of his failure, and the trappings of
> royalty, of kingship, are simply trappings to
> make him more splendid so that he was worthy
> of being selected by the gods, by Olympus,
> as an opponent, that man couldn't cope with
> him so it would take a god to do it, to cast
> him down.[21]

5

A study of Euripides' work would prove that he too agrees
that "the common man is as apt a subject for tragedy in its
highest sense as kings were."[22]

More particularly, one may note that the basic focus
and characteristics of Faulkner's tragic vision reflect the
basic focus and characteristics that a study of the work
of Euripides reveals.[23] Both tragedians have manifested
an essential humanism, a technique concerned with the
psychological understanding of the inner conflict of man's
divided soul, and a skeptical and questioning approach
to their respective tragic worlds which fail in various
ways to measure up to their ideals. By creating worlds
which mirror the lives of their contemporaries, not as
they think they are, but as they really are, they both
manifest a tragic vision by which they see man "in all
his relationships and possibilities as well as his
limitations."[24] And although they both see that these
relationships and limitations do often produce a world
which cannot be viewed any way but pessimistically, they
do, by one means or another, leave their audiences with a
feeling of affirmation and the knowledge that man must --
and will--prevail and endure.

FOOTNOTES

1. Richard B. Sewall, The Vision of Tragedy (New Haven: Yale University Press, 1959), p. 133.

2. Sewall, p. 134.

3. Ernest G. Griffin, "William Faulkner and the Tragic Ritual" (unpublished Master's thesis, Dept. of English, Columbia University, June, 1951), p. 2.

4. Griffin, p. 30.
Griffin (p. 9) explains the tragic pattern as that which makes us feel the mysterious and ultimately indivisible flow of life and the harmony of the universe behind the struggle of the human will.

5. Griffin, p. 50.

6. Leonard Mikules, "The Road to William Faulkner" (unpublished Ph.D. dissertation, Dept. of English, University of California at Los Angeles, 1957), p. 250.
R. W. Flint in "Faulkner as Elegist," The Hudson Review, VII (Summer, 1954), 257, speaks of Faulkner's novels in the tradition of "high tragi-comedy in Western art."

7. George Marion O'Donnell, "Faulkner's Mythology," The Kenyon Review, I (Summer, 1939), 299.

8. René Leibowitz, "L'art tragique de William Faulkner, Cahiers du Sud, XIX (November, 1940), 503.

9. Cecil B. Williams, "William Faulkner and the Nobel Prize Awards," Faulkner Studies, I (Summer, 1952), 19.
Other recent Faulkner critics who have categorized many of his novels as tragedies and discussed his protagonists as tragic heroes are:
Hyatt H. Waggoner, William Faulkner: From Jefferson to the World (n.p.): The University of Kentucky Press, 1959),

6

NOTE: The forms for the footnotes and the bibliography of this sample paper (written 1961) follow the style in the first MLA Style Sheet. The new form recommended in the MLA revision of 1970 is the form in STEPS 4 and 9 of this revised edition of *10 Steps*. Both are "correct."

Mary Cooper Robb, William Faulkner (Pittsburgh: 7
University of Pittsburgh Press, 1957), and
Olga W. Vickery, The Novels of William Faulkner (Baton
Rouge: Louisiana State University Press, 1959).

10. Cedric H. Whitman's study, Sophocles (Cambridge:
Harvard University Press, 1951), for example, attempts to
show the essential tenets of humanism in the work of
Sophocles. However, the other critics of classical drama,
almost without exception, have emphasized the fact that
the characteristics of humanism are found most obviously
in the works of Euripides.

11. L. R. Lind, "Introduction," Ten Greek Plays in
Contemporary Translations, L. R. Lind, ed. (Boston:
Houghton Mifflin Co., 1957), p. xxi.

12. Moses Hadas, "Introduction," Ten Plays by
Euripides, Moses Hadas and John McLean, eds. (New York:
Bantam Books, 1960), pp. vii-viii.

Cf. Edith Hamilton, The Greek Way to Western Civiliza-
tion (New York: The New American Library, 1930), p. 198, and
F. L. Lucas, Tragedy in Relation to Aristotle's
Poetics (London: The Hogarth Press, 1928), p. 117.

13. F. L. Lucas, Euripides and His Influence (Boston:
Marshall Jones Co., 1923), p. 175.

14. See Aristotle, De Poetica, trans. Ingram Bywater,
6, 7, and 14, The Basic Works of Aristotle, Richard McKeon,
ed. (New York: Random House, 1941), pp. 1460-63, 1467-69.

15. See Arthur Miller, "Tragedy and the Common Man,"
The New York Times, February 27, 1949, II, 1, 3.

16. S. H. Butcher, Aristotle's Theory of Poetry and
Fine Art (London: Macmillan and Co., Ltd., 1927), p. 219.

17. Miller, II, 3.

18. Miller, II, 3.

19. Miller, II, 1.

20. Miller, II, 3.

21. Frederick L. Gwynn and Joseph L. Blotner, eds.,
Faulkner in the University (Charlottesville: University
of Virginia Press, 1959), p. 51.

22. Miller, II, 1.

23. The characteristics and focus of the work of
Euripides will be investigated and explained for the reader
in Chapter I.

24. C. Carter Colwell, "The Persistence of Tragedy,"
Modern Age, IV (Summer, 1960), 328.
Sewall, p. 132, makes this a requisite for tragedy.

BIBLIOGRAPHY

Aristotle. De Poetica. Trans. Ingram Bywater. The Basic
    Works of Aristotle. Richard McKeon, ed. New York:
    Random House, 1941. Pp. 1453-87.

Butcher, S. H. Aristotle's Theory of Poetry and Fine Art.
    London: Macmillan and Co., Ltd., 1927.

Colwell, C. Carter. "The Persistence of Tragedy," Modern
    Age, IV (Summer, 1960), 326-28.

Flint, R. W. "Faulkner as Elegist," The Hudson Review, VII
    (Summer, 1954), 246-57.

Griffin, Ernest G. "William Faulkner and the Tragic Ritual."
    Unpublished Master's thesis, Dept. of English, Columbia
    University, June, 1951.

Gwynn, Frederick L. and Joseph L. Blotner (eds.). Faulkner
    in the University. Charlottesville: University of
    Virginia Press, 1959.

Hadas, Moses. "Introduction," Ten Plays by Euripides,
    Moses Hadas and John McLean, eds. New York: Bantam
    Books, 1960. Pp. vii-xix.

Hamilton, Edith. The Greek Way to Western Civilization.
    New York: The New American Library, 1930.

Leibowitz, René. "L'art tragique de William Faulkner,"
    Cahiers du Sud, XIX (November, 1940), 502-8.

Lind, L. R. "Introduction," Ten Greek Plays in Contemporary
    Translations, L. R. Lind, ed. Boston: Houghton Mifflin
    Co., 1957. Pp. ix-xxviii.

Lucas, F. L. Euripides and His Influence. Boston: Marshall
    Jones Co., 1923.

_____. Tragedy in Relation to Aristotle's Poetics.
    London: The Hogarth Press, 1928.

Mikules, Leonard. "The Road to William Faulkner." Unpub-
    lished Ph.D. dissertation, Dept. of English, Univer-
    sity of California at Los Angeles, 1957.

Miller, Arthur. "Tragedy and the Common Man," The New York
    Times, February 27, 1949, II, 1, 3.

9

O'Donnell, George Marion. "Faulkner's Mythology," Kenyon Review, I (Summer, 1939), 285-99.

Robb, Mary Cooper. William Faulkner. Pittsburgh: University of Pittsburgh Press, 1957.

Sewall, Richard B. The Vision of Tragedy. New Haven: Yale University Press, 1959.

Vickery, Olga W. The Novels of William Faulkner. Baton Rouge: Louisiana State University Press, 1959.

Waggoner, Hyatt H. William Faulkner: From Jefferson to the World. (n.p.): University of Kentucky Press, 1959.

Whitman, Cedric H. Sophocles. Cambridge: Harvard University Press, 1951.

Williams, Cecil B. "William Faulkner and the Nobel Prize Awards," Faulkner Studies, I (Summer, 1952), 17-19.

Plagiarism: A Step to Avoid *

The only problem of composition that is unique to the research paper is this: you must use and work with the ideas and words of other scholars. Before you are ready for this privilege and its attendant responsibility, you must understand and remember that an idea, though not a tangible article, is just as much the property of another as his car or his clothes; often it is much more valuable. You must not use it without properly acknowledging your indebtedness. This acknowledgement, far from weakening your paper, will in fact add value and authority to your writing.

If every student understood clearly what plagiarism is, the following illustrations would not be necessary. However, the question of what is honest and what is dishonest use of source material is one which plagues many students; many of the unwary and uninformed have suffered serious consequences academically. As with the entire philosophical question of honesty, there are various degrees of plagiarism. If these examples and your own conscience are inadequate guides, consult the person who is guiding your research paper work.

Word–for–word plagiarism

There are two novels of William Faulkner, *The Sound and the Fury* and *Light in August,* which provide a tremendous stimulus for thought. If one knows the characteristics of classical tragedy, he cannot read these novels without an awareness of their basic similarity to the tragic form in spite of Joseph Wood Krutch's idea to the contrary ex-

* The illustrations for this section are based on the Preface reproduced on page 50. It is also reproduced as part of the explanation for the Paraphrase (pages 112-114) at the end of this section on Plagiarism.

pressed in his article "The Tragic Fallacy" concerning the inability of modern writers to create tragedy because of their lack of tragic faith. But it seems obvious that Arthur Miller's concept (expressed in "Tragedy and the Common Man") which recognizes the need for tragedy to be concerned with the spirit and heart of the ordinary man will provide one with enough reason to the contrary to permit a student of modern fiction to substantiate an argument for the existence of tragedy in the twentieth century. Furthermore, the best prose of William Faulkner seems to qualify him as a modern tragedian.

COMMENT: Transposing or substituting a few words will not create a paraphrase. In this example, after saying "There are two novels" instead of "Two of the novels," the writer of this nearly verbatim piece of plagiarism simply omitted phrases with the personal pronoun or reworded some passages: "provided" was changed to "will provide one with"; "average" became "ordinary"; "spirit and heart" merely reverses Miller's phrase so carefully quoted in the source. As written, this passage is almost purely a word-for-word copy of the source, retaining even the sentence structure and organization of the original. Even the use of a footnote could not save this paragraph from being condemned.

Patchwork plagiarism

A tremendous stimulus for thought may be found in two of the novels of Faulkner, *The Sound and the Fury* and *Light in August*. Even a rudimentary study of Faulkner may compel the student who knows the character-

istics of classical tragedy to make a study of |Faulkner's*|
best novels to see whether they have any basic similarity to the tragic form. Joseph Wood Krutch, in "The
Tragic Fallacy," discusses the inability of modern writers
to create true tragedy because of their lack of tragic faith.
But to substantiate an argument for the existence of tragedy
in the twentieth century, one may use the concept Arthur
Miller expressed in "Tragedy and the Common Man";
there he states the need for tragedy to be concerned with
the heart and spirit of the average man. Indeed, the best
prose of William Faulkner does seem to qualify him as a
modern tragedian; to prove that statement is the purpose
of this paper.

COMMENT: * Changing a single word in a passage
otherwise quoted verbatim does not
make a paraphrase. The starred passage
would still need to be in quotation
marks and footnoted; the change(s) you
make will go in square brackets, as do
all editorial changes and additions; ellipsis marks are used between two passages
not connected in the source being quoted. Thus for the starred sentence above:

A study of modern literature may
compel the student who knows "the
characteristics of classical tragedy . . .
to make a study of Faulkner's best
novels."

The footnote number would then follow the quotation marks.

When whole phrases are lifted out and
are put into a framework of your own
wording or into a "different" arrangement of the original, the result is also
called plagiarism. In the example above,
the underlined phrases are verbatim

from the original. Though you would never be expected to put quotation marks merely around such phrases as "the average man" and "to make a study" and "the best prose" since they are part of our common idiom, you could not write such a sentence as the fourth one above and call it your own. This "rearrangement" is not really a paraphrasing. The first clause of the last sentence might be called a paraphrase but would still need a footnote; the clause after the semicolon certainly adds nothing to the "content" of the paragraph. If all underlined phrases were in quotation marks, the paragraph would resemble an old-fashioned patchwork quilt. It would also be quite unreadable and certainly not original.

"Lifting out the perfect phrases"

After a rudimentary study of Faulkner, I found a tremendous stimulus for thought in two of his novels, *The Sound and the Fury* and *Light in August*. Having studied the characteristics of classical tragedy, I came to see that these novels have a real and basic similarity to the tragic form. Some critics, it is true, think modern writers are unable to create tragedy because of their lack of tragic faith. However, in order to substantiate an argument for the existence of tragedy in the twentieth century, I should like to use Arthur Miller's concept, which recognizes the need for tragedy to be concerned with "the heart and spirit of the average man."[1] It is true that J. W. Krutch in "The Tragic Fallacy" says modern writers cannot create tragedy. But there seems to be a widespread misconception that tragedy is allied to pessimism. The truth is, tragedy implies more optimism in its author than does comedy. In fact, true tragedy ought to reinforce the reader's brightest opinions of mankind. Therefore I shall try to prove that the best prose of William Faulkner qualifies him as a modern tragedian who has a basically optimistic view of the human animal.

[1] Arthur Miller, "Tragedy and the Common Man," *The New York Times*, February 27, 1949, II, 3.*

COMMENT: Though more subtle and clever, this kind of plagiarism is similar to the patchwork illustration above. The "perfect phrases" irresistible to the writer here are underlined so you may spot them easily.

The words in boxes might be called paraphrases, but could not be used without a footnote. The phrasing "a basically optimistic view of the human animal" is certainly Miller's idea and though paraphrased must be documented as having been quoted by Hoffman.

Two other serious errors were made in this paragraph:

* 1. Miller was cited in a footnote as if his article were a source used by the writer. (If you did not read the article, you may not cite it.)

2. Not content with "lifting" material from the Preface, the writer here has copied the words "allied to pessimism" from Miller so carefully quoted in Hoffman's footnotes.

Paraphrase

PREFACE

Two of the novels of William Faulkner, *The Sound and*

The Sound and the Fury and Light in August

the *Fury* and *Light in August,* have provided for me, as

by William Faulkner are very stimulating

for many other readers, a tremendous stimulus for thought.

novels. Even a casual reading of them

After a rudimentary study of Faulkner, I felt compelled to

may stimulate one to make a further study

make a study of his best novels. Knowing the characteristics

of his best novels. There is a close similarity

of classical tragedy, I could not read these novels without

between these novels and dramatic tragedy.

an awareness of their basic similarity to the tragic form in

In "The Tragic Fallacy"

spite of the idea that Joseph Wood Krutch expresses to the

Joseph Wood Krutch says that modern writers

contrary in "The Tragic Fallacy" concerning the inability

cannot write tragedy because they have

of modern writers to create tragedy because of their lack

no faith.

of tragic faith. It seemed obvious to me that Arthur Miller's

But Arthur Miller,

concept, expressed in "Tragedy and the Common Man,"

in "Tragedy and the Common Man," says

which recognizes the need for tragedy to be concerned with

that tragedy should deal with the life and

"the heart and spirit of the average man," provided enough

the soul of the common man; he also

reason to the contrary to permit me to substantiate an argu-

maintains that the writer of tragedy is

ment for the existence of tragedy in the twentieth century.

actually more optimistic than the writer
of comedy. If so then it is easy to
argue that tragedy can and does
exist in the twentieth century.

Furthermore, I was convinced that the best prose of Wil-

Certainly the best novels of William Faulkner

liam Faulkner qualified him as a modern tragedian.

seem to prove that he is at least one modern writer who can be called a tragedian in the classical sense.

[1] Joseph Wood Krutch, "The Tragic Fallacy," *The Modern Temper: A Study and a Confession* (New York: Harcourt, Brace and Co., 1956), pp. 79-97.

[2] Arthur Miller, "Tragedy and the Common Man," *The New York Times*, February 27, 1949, II,3, states that "there is a misconception of tragedy . . . . It is the idea that tragedy is of necessity allied to pessimism . . . . In truth tragedy implies more optimism in its author than does comedy . . . [and] ought to be the reinforcement of the onlooker's brightest opinions of the human animal."

[2] *Arthur Miller, "Tragedy and the Common Man," The New York Times, February 27, 1949, II, 3, quoted by Roberta G. Hoffman, in "Tragedy: from Athens to Yoknapatawpha" (unpublished Master's thesis Department of English, Columbia University, 1961), p. iv.*

COMMENT: This a paraphrase, for the writer here has followed the source, sentence by sentence and idea by idea, but has used his own words. There is value in doing this (see the reasons listed above card F on page 58), but remember that you must not alter the sense of the original.

Also remember: although the words in a paraphrase (or a précis, *q. v.*) may truly be your own, the thoughts and opinions are not; therefore you must acknowledge your indebtedness to the thinking of the original writer by one of three methods:

1. Put a footnote number after the passage and in a footnote give the source. See STEP 9.
2. Use an informal in-text documentation. See page 79–80, 89–90.
3. Assuming that you have already given a footnote for this paraphrased PREFACE, give the author credit in a phrase such as "to paraphrase Hoffman's thesis, —" or "As Hoffman says in her Preface, – – " and in a footnote give simply the page number. (See 9 on page 89.)

REMEMBER: Of the four examples above, only the paraphrase could be used without quotation marks, and even it would require documentation in a footnote. THE OTHER EXAMPLES WOULD BE CALLED PLAGIARISM *EVEN WITH* DOCUMENTATION.

The Library: A Step to Master

Using the Library for Books and Other Communications Media.

The library is the most valuable storehouse of information on almost every subject for anyone doing research. It is essential, therefore, to become familiar with the tools in your library and to make use of as many of them as your time affords.

1. **The Card Catalogue**

   Any student should consider the card catalogue as his most valuable index. When you locate a card for a book you want, it is essential to copy the entire call number accurately, since it is the most important mark of identification for locating any book.

2. **The Reference Rooms**

   Become familiar with the basic reference texts in your particular subject. The periodical indexes, special indexes, bibliographies, special encyclopedias (see pp. 14–17) are in the reference room of the library. Ask at the information desk to find out whether or not the library has reference rooms for different subjects or whether all references may be found in one place.

3. **Special Sections**

   In larger libraries there are often special rooms for collections of bibliographies, circulating art prints and slides, periodicals, audio-visual aids, phonograph records, tapes, pamphlets, rare books and folios, newspapers, reserve books, dissertations and other unpublished manuscripts, maps, and other special materials, each of which may have its own separate catalogue or listing; hence it is important for you to check these various sections in your particular library as you search for relevant materials.

4. Films and Filmstrips

Many libraries afford students the opportunity of previewing films and filmstrips; often, arrangements must be made in advance for this privilege.

5. Pamphlets

Pamphlets are a valuable source of additional current information on any subject. Often they are circulated, although they will not be found listed in the card catalogue. Even a little pamphlet can contain great ideas.

6. Microfilms and Microcards

Microfilms and microtexts have enabled libraries to store and mail copies of books which would not otherwise be available. Microfilm reading machines are easy to use and very interesting; you may even find that the machine helps you to keep awake between pages. Microtexts require the use of a microprint reading machine which is also simple to handle; it enables a library to have an entire work on a single card. In a busy library, be sure to make arrangements in advance for the use of these miraculous machines.

7. Records and Tapes

Although many students may not be aware of it, music is not the only material that is available on phonograph records and tapes. You should check these for recordings of lectures and readings on every subject, since some of these may not be available in other media.

8. Newspapers

All issues of the most important newspapers are available on microfilm; they are often listed in the holding file of a periodical room.

9. Periodicals

Many periodical indexes are available in the reference room of the library. (See pp. 14-15.) After you have found the source of an article that interests you, check the holding file of periodicals to find out if the periodical you need is available in your library. Issues of periodicals published in the same year have the same volume number and are eventually bound together in the same volume; so if you need several issues with the same volume number (of a bound periodical), you need to ask or look for only one bound volume. Often you can arrange to borrow those that are not available in your library, but this entails using the interlibrary loan service discussed under 12 d below.

10. Picture File

Mounted magazine pictures, commercially prepared study prints, and pictorial maps are often available through the library. These can be valuable aids in many areas of research. Art prints are often available on loan for you to enjoy at home or in your own room for a considerable length of time.

11. Stack Privileges

Depending on the regulations of each individual library, some students have the privilege of going directly to the library stacks, a privilege which will enable them to look at all the works in sections (or call numbers) related to their research subjects. If you have this privilege, this chance to browse will reveal material that you might not have found in the card catalogue. It is important to use the indexes of the various books that seem relevant in order to ascertain their value to your project.

12. Special Services

Your library is often equipped to offer you many special services:

 a. Renewal of books you have not finished using,

 b. "Holding" a book that someone else has taken out of the library. If you request a "hold" on a book, your library will notify you when it is returned to the library and before it is returned to the library. It is important to respond quickly to a notice that a "hold" book is waiting for you, because your library may have a time limit on this service.

 c. Xerox or copying machines are usually available for you to use in "copying" or duplicating material from a book in the library. Be aware of the copyright laws, however, as only a limited amount of material is legally available for copying.

 d. Most libraries subscribe to an interlibrary loan service which makes available most of the world's materials, even those not in your library. Materials obtained through this service are usually borrowed for a very limited time, so it is wise to find out how long it will take for the material to reach you and how long you may keep it.

  There are, of course, many ways in which you will encounter the names of books that you think will be valuable for your research. Usually you will find them in bibliographies by other researchers or referred to in footnotes or appendixes in your sources. Then you should check the *National Union Catalog*, which your librarian will have and with which you can locate books in hundreds of American libraries. Through the interlibrary loan service you can usually obtain the books you need. Winifred Gregory's *Union List of Serials,* though not quite as complete or up-to-date, also serves the same purpose: it helps you locate periodicals in other libraries. You can find films listed in the *Union List of Microfilms* and *Newspapers on Microfilms.*

   e. Typewriters are available for student use in most libraries and are usually coin-operated.

13. The Reference Librarian

The reference librarian is always a busy person, but when all else fails he is the one who is professionally trained to help you locate materials and use the library to its greatest potential. Solicit his help only after you have tried to help yourself, but do not hesitate to ask for help when you honestly need it.

Research Terms Defined

Research writing, like any other specialized activity, has its own jargon. The following are terms frequently used by people in discussing research:

abridgment: a condensation of the author's original work (expurgated text).

acknowledgment: recognition made of indebtedness to another.

annotated bibliography: a bibliography with comments about each source, telling how inclusive it is, how valuable it is, what the author does and what his purpose is, and so on.

authority: a writer whose work and opinions are generally accepted as final and reliable.

autobiography: the writer's own account of his life.

bibliography: a list of books, articles, and other material about a single subject, idea, person, and so forth.

biography: a writer's account of the life story of another. There are three types: straight, fictional, and critical.

brackets: the punctuation marks [ ] used only within a quoted passage to enclose additions in your own words (called editorial comment, insertion, or interpolation) explaining a word or giving information needed by the reader.

Brackets may be drawn in black ink if the typewriter has no brackets. NEVER use unnecessary brackets: "He [Aristotle] wrote an early definition of tragedy"; simply write this: Aristotle "wrote an early definition of tragedy." Parentheses are different and have a different function.

card catalogue: a card file listing alphabetically all books in a library.

Usually each book is listed under author, book title, and subject.

cross reference: words or symbols which refer the reader to other places where information about an idea may be found.

Cross references are used in card catalogues, footnotes, indexes, and bibliographies.

compile (compilation, compiler): to combine related material. The one who does the combining is a compiler; the result is a compilation.

dedication: a page of tribute by the writer to one he admires or feels indebted to or wants to honor.

dissertation: a long, involved, and formal exposition on some serious or scholarly subject.

In academic circles, the word is usually reserved for those papers written by a candidate for the Doctor's degree; the word *thesis* indicates the paper written by a candidate for the Master's degree.

document: to acknowledge indebtedness for an idea or fact. It is necessary to document the source of any critical opinion (and some facts) ; see the section on footnotes, STEP 9.

ellipsis: an omission within quoted material indicated by three periods with a space before, after, and between periods (. . .).

The ellipsis marks may indicate the omission of a single word or of whole sentences, but you must never omit words which would change the essential, intended meaning of the quoted material. It is illogical to use an ellipsis to open or to close a quoted passage; hence it would never come immediately aften an opening quotation mark nor immediately before the closing quotation mark; it should be used only to show an omission within a quoted passage. Use a fourth period only before a new sentence which begins after an ellipsis within the quoted passage.

file: frequently misused as a substitute for the proper term, *card catalogue.*

The word *file* is properly used to refer to some special library file such as the Vertical File which contains temporarily interesting leaflets, pamphlets, newspaper and magazine clippings, illustrations, and so on that are not permanently classified and filed but are put in standing (vertical) files and removed when the interest fades: as one librarian put it, "temporary stuff and current junk."

foreword: a note from the author at the front of a book.

Current practice reveals that there is some confusion about the exact distinctions between the sections called *foreword, preface,* and *introduction;* however, by whatever name it may be called, this section sets forth an explanation by the author of his intended purpose, his reason for writing, and any information or background he thinks will be needed by the reader.

interpolate: to insert an idea or material or information where it should logically go in the organization of the writing.

introduction: a section which follows the table of contents and introduces the work that follows. See *foreword* above.

pagination: the system for numbering pages of a manuscript or book.

parentheses: the punctuation marks ( ) used to enclose your own explanatory material or words interpolated into a sentence or phrase of your own.

Brackets (*q.v.*) enclose material more foreign to the context than that put in parentheses; avoid the overuse of either.

plagiarism: a literary word for the thievery of style, ideas, or phrasing.

Plagiarism ranges from the theft of a single word to the deliberate copying (without quotation marks) of a whole passage; it can be avoided by careful note taking and footnoting (*q.v.*); everything not documented must be your own original idea and phrasing. You are not writing original sentences of your own if you merely arrange into a new order or sentence pattern some select phrases and sentences taken without quotation marks from your sources. See section entitled *Plagiarism: A Step to Avoid,* pp. 107–115.

primary source: the literature, the work, manuscript, journal, letters, and so on as originally written.

A secondary source is a work written about an original source; a primary source in connection with one subject might be a secondary source in connection with another subject.

. For example, a novel by Faulkner would be a primary source for a paper about Faulkner or the novel in America and so on; the preface from a Master's thesis (like the one on p. 50) would be a primary source for a paper on the writing of theses in American colleges and universities, but it would be a secondary source for a paper on Faulkner.

preface: a note from the author which comes before (some put it after) the table of contents or outline.

The preface is frequently followed by a page of acknowledgments; see *foreword* above.

rough draft: the first and any subsequent writing before the paper is put in final form.

Rough drafts are subject to drastic and sometimes numerous revisions.

reference or reference book: any source being read for information.

The number and quality of your references will in

large measure determine the quality of your finished paper.

scan: to make a cursory reading of material in order to evaluate it and decide how to read it.

secondary source: a criticism or evaluation of an original piece of writing.

See *primary source* above.

slug (label, tag): the label on a notecard written above the top line and immediately after the identifying symbol.

It may be taken from or may suggest ideas for the outline units.

thesis: the simple statement of opinion which the entire work is designed to support.

See complete explanation and examples in STEP 3.

Library Classification Systems

The "call numbers" on the cards in the card catalogue and on the backs of books usually follow the Library of Congress system or the Dewey decimal system. The latter is more often used by college libraries.

All branches of knowledge are divided into ten numbered parts according to hundreds which are then further divided into specific areas of knowledge. The number on the first line is the call number; below it are other lines indicating the code used for author, a particular work, the edition, the number of copies on hand, and so on. The numbers below indicate ways the number on the first line may appear.

000	General Works
100	Philosophy
200	Religion
300	Social Sciences
400	Language (Philology)
500	Pure Science
600	Useful Arts
700	Fine Arts
800	Literature
900	History

These parts are further divided; the second number in the 800's indicates the country or language of the literature.

810	American Literature in English
820	English and Old English
830	Germanic Literature
840	French, Provençal, Catalan
850	Italian, Rumanian
860	Spanish,Portuguese

870   Latin and Italic Literature
880   Classical and Modern Greek
890   Other Literatures

The third number indicates types of literature.

811   American Poetry
812   American Drama
813   American Fiction
814   American Essays
815   American Oratory
816   American Letters
817   American Satire and Humor
818   American Miscellany
819   Canadian (used rarely)

After three numbers, there is a period; the number immediately following indicates the time or period in literature.

811.1   Colonial Poetry
811.2   Post-Revolutionary Poetry
811.3   Middle 19th Century Poetry
811.4   Later 19th Century Poetry
811.5   Twentieth Century Poetry

After the period and a zero, the number indicates the type of literature.

811.06   Descriptive Poetry in American Poetry
811.07   Satire and Humor in American Poetry
811.08   Collections of American Poetry
811.09   History of American Poetry

Other numbers indicate further classification, but these are the main ones you will need or want to know. If you know them and if you are given access to the stacks in the library, you can find books for yourself.

THE LIBRARY OF CONGRESS CLASSIFICATION SYSTEM

The Library of Congress system divides all fields of knowledge into twenty main groups:

A   General Works–Polygraphy
B   Philosophy–Religion
C   History–Auxiliary Sciences
D   History–Topography (except America)
E-F American History and Topography
G   Geography–Anthropology
H   Social Sciences
J   Political Science
K   Law
L   Education
M   Music
N   Fine Arts
P   Language and Literature
Q   Science
R   Medicine
S   Agriculture–Plant and Animal Husbandry
T   Technology
U   Military Science
V   Naval Science
Z   Bibliography and Library Science

Reference Materials and Guides

Most research will start in the reference room of your library; there you will find many volumes written not to be read, but to be used as guides to general and to specialized articles and books about all fields of knowledge. These indexes and general reference books are guides only; they do not contain material you will read; they will not be a part of your bibliography. Quite literally, they are tools which you must learn to use, and no amount of explanation will replace experience and an active imagination; hence the list below contains only the names of a few reference guides and is not annotated.

GENERAL WORKS

There are numerous atlases, dictionaries, and encyclopedias which are too familiar to the average student to need listing here.

GUIDES TO REFERENCE SOURCES

Barton, Mary N., comp. *Reference Books, a Brief Guide for Students and Other Users of the Library,* 7th ed. Baltimore: Enoch Pratt Free Library, 1970.

Courtney, Winifred F. *The Reader's Advisor,* 11th ed. 2 vols. New York: Bowker, 1968.

Murphey, Robert W. *How and Where to Look It Up: A Guide to Standard Sources of Information.* New York: McGraw-Hill, 1958.

Vitale, Philip H. *Basic Tools of Research.* Woodbury, New York: Barron's, 1968.

Walford, J. *Guide to Reference Material.* 3 vols. London: The Library Association, 1968. (A reprint.)

Winchell, Constance M. *Guide to Reference Books,* 8th ed. Chicago: American Library Association, 1967. Supplements 1965-1966, 1967-1968.

NOTE: The above guides give more detailed information about possible sources than you will find in some indexes (such as those which follow).

BIBLIOGRAPHIES AND SUPPLEMENTS
TO THE CARD CATALOGUE

Besterman, Theodore. *A World Bibliography of Bibliographies,* 4th ed. 5 vols. Geneva: Societas Bibliographica, 1965-1966.

Bibliographic Index: A Cumulative Bibliography of Bibliographies. New York: H. W. Wilson, 1934 to date.

The Cumulative Book Index. New York: H. W. Wilson, 1928 to date. (For books in print in English prior to 1928, see *The United States Catalog,* 4th ed. New York: H. W. Wilson, 1928.)

Essay and General Literature Index. New York: H. W. Wilson, 1934 to date.

A Guide to the Study of the United States of America. Washington, D. C.: Library of Congress, 1960.

Monthly Catalog of United States Government Publications. Washington, D. C.: Government Printing Office, 1895 to date.

BIOGRAPHICAL REFERENCE BOOKS AND DICTIONARIES

Biography Index. New York: H. W. Wilson, 1946 to date.

Chamber's Biographical Dictionary. New York: St. Martin's Press, 1961.

Current Biography. New York: H. W. Wilson, 1940 to date.

Dictionary of American Biography. 22 volumes, index, and supplements. New York: Scribner, 1928-1944.

Webster's Biographical Dictionary. Springfield, Mass.: G. & C. Merriam, 1970.

Who's Who. New York: Macmillan, 1849 to date.

Who's Who in America. Chicago: A. N. Marquis, 1899 to date.

REFERENCE BOOKS AND INDEXES ON VARIOUS SUBJECTS

It is almost impossible to draw absolute lines dividing ideas and subjects, to say that one idea concerns just one and no other area of man's thinking; it is also impossible to define exactly the line distinguishing the subject matter in all the books in a library. The list below therefore makes arbitrary divisions for the sake of convenience.

The fine arts and the humanities

Art Index. New York: H. W. Wilson, 1929 to date.

Bartlett, John. *Familiar Quotations,* 14th ed. Boston: Little, Brown, 1968.

Blanck, Jacob, comp. *Bibliography of American Literature.* 5 vols. New Haven: Yale University Press, 1955-1969. (Other volumes in process.)

Burke, W. J., and Will D. Howe. *American Authors and Books,* augmented and revised by Irving R. Weiss. New York: Crown, 1962.

Cambridge Bibliography of English Literature. 5 vols. Cambridge: Cambridge University Press, 1941-1957.

Gardner, Helen. *Art Through the Ages,* 5th ed. New York: Harcourt, Brace, Javanovich, 1970.

Granger's Index to Poetry, 5th ed. New York: Columbia University Press, 1962. Supplement, 1960-64.

Grove's Dictionary of Music and Musicians, 5th ed. 9 vols. New York: St. Martin's Press, 1954. Supplement, 1961.

Hopper, Vincent F., and Bernard D. N. Grebanier. *Bibliography of European Literature.* Woodbury, New York: Barron's, 1954.

Index to Art Periodicals, compiled in Ryerson Library, The Art Institute of Chicago. 11 vols. Boston: G. K. Hall, 1962.

M.L.A. Bibliography. New York: Modern Language Association of America, 1929 to date.

The National Union Catalog (motion pictures and filmstrips) . Library of Congress Catalogs 1963-67. 5 vols. Ann Arbor, Michigan: Edwards Brothers, 1967.

Ottemiller, John H. *Index to Plays in Collections,* 4th ed. Metuchen, New Jersey: Scarecrow Press, 1964.

Play Index. New York: H. W. Wilson, 1963. (Formerly *Index to Plays,* 1800-1926, Ina Firkins, comp.)

Schirmer's Guide to Books on Music and Musicians. New York: Schirmer, 1951.

Union List of Microfilms. Cumulation 1949-1959. 2 vols. Ann Arbor, Michigan: Edwards Brothers, 1961.

The sciences

GENERAL WORKS

Applied Science and Technology Index. New York: H. W. Wilson, 1958. (Formerly *Industrial Arts Index,* 1913-1958.)

Hawkins, Reginald R. *Scientific, Medical and Technical Books Published in the United States of America.* Washington, D. C.: National Research Council, 1958.

Sarton, George. *A Guide to the History of Science.* New York: Ronald, 1952.

BIOLOGY AND AGRICULTURE

Biological and Agricultural Index. New York: H. W. Wilson, 1964 to date.

Yearbook of Agriculture. Washington, D. C.: U. S. Department of Agriculture, 1894 to date. (Each year a different subject is covered.)

ENGINEERING

Dalton, Blanche H. *Sources of Engineering Information.*
Berkeley: University of California Press, 1948.
The Engineering Index. New York: Engineering Index,
Inc., 1970. (Volume 1 — 1884; volume 69 — 1970)

MATHEMATICS, CHEMISTRY, AND PHYSICS

Crane, Evan J., Austin M. Patterson, and Eleanor B. Marr.
A Guide to the Literature of Chemistry, 2nd ed. New
York: John Wiley & Sons, 1957.
Mellon, Melvin G. *Chemical Publications,* 4th ed. New
York: McGraw-Hill, 1965.
Parke, Nathan G. *Guide to the Literature of Mathematics
and Physics,* 2nd ed. New York: McGraw-Hill, 1958.

The social sciences

GENERAL WORKS

Clark, J. A. *Research Materials in the Social Sciences.* Madi-
son, Wisconsin: University of Wisconsin Press, 1959.
Hoselitz, Berthold F. *A Reader's Guide to the Social
Sciences,* rev. ed. Glencoe, Illinois: Free Press, 1970.
Social Sciences & Humanities Index. New York: H. W.
Wilson, 1907 to date. (Formerly *The International
Index to Periodical Literature,* 1907-1966. Name
changed in 1966 with volume 20.)
White, Carl M. *Sources of Information in the Social Sci-
ences: A Guide to the Literature.* Totowa, New Jersey:
Bedminster Press, 1964.

BUSINESS AND ECONOMICS

Coman, Edwin T. *Sources of Business Information,* rev. ed. New York: Prentice-Hall, 1964.

Horton, Byrne J., and others. *Dictionary of Modern Economics.* Washington, D. C.: Public Affairs Press, 1948.

Manley, Marian C. *Business Information: How to Find and Use It.* New York: Harper, 1955.

EDUCATION

Alexander, Carter, and Arvid J. Burke. *Documentation in Education.* New York: Bureau of Publications, Teachers College, Columbia University, 1967.

Education Index. New York: H. W. Wilson, 1929 to date.

Encyclopaedia of Educational Research, 4th ed. New York: Macmillan, 1969.

HISTORY AND POLITICAL SCIENCE AND SOCIOLOGY

Beers, Henry P. *Bibliographies in American History,* rev. and enl. ed. New York: Cooper Square Press, 1960.

Brock, Clifton. *The Literature of Political Science.* New York: R. R. Bowker, 1969.

Clark, George K. *Guide for Research Students Working on Historical Subjects,* 2nd ed. Cambridge: Cambridge University Press, 1968.

Dutcher, George Matthew, and others, eds. *Guide to Historical Literature.* New York: Macmillan, 1949. (A reissue.)

Langer, William, and others, comps. and eds. *Encyclopaedia of World History,* 4th ed. Boston: Houghton Mifflin, 1968.

Statesman's Year-Book. New York: Macmillan, 1864 to date.

RELIGION, PHILOSOPHY, AND PSYCHOLOGY

Baldwin, James M. *Dictionary of Philosophy and Psychology*. 3 vols. in 4. New York: Smith, 1925. (A reissue in 1949.)

Encyclopedia of Philosophy. 8 vols. New York: Macmillan, 1967.

Ferm, Vergilius. *Encyclopedia of Religion*. New York: Philosophical Library, 1945.

Hastings, James, ed. *Encyclopaedia of Religion and Ethics*. 12 vols. and index. New York: Scribner's, 1951 (?).

List of Books in Psychology, 3rd ed. Cambridge: Harvard University Press, 1964.

Runes, Dagobert D. *Dictionary of Philosophy*. New York: Philosophical Library, 1942.

Warren, Howard C. *Dictionary of Psychology*. New York: Houghton Mifflin, 1934.

Abbreviations

anon.	anonymous
bk., bks.	book(s)
c., ca.	*circa:* "about"; for approximate dates (c. 1884, ca. 1884)
cf.	*confer:* "compare"; not a synonym for "see"
chap., ch., chs.	chapter(s)
col., cols.	column(s)
comp.	compiler, compiled, compiled by
ed., eds.	editor(s), edition(s), or edited by
e.g.	*exempli gratia:* "for example"
et al.	*et alii:* "and others"
et seq.	*et sequens:* "and the following" (or ff., which is shorter)
	example

f., ff.	and the following page(s) (pp. 79f. or pp. 79ff.)
fig., figs.	figure(s)
ibid.	*ibidem:* "in the same place as quoted above"; refers to title in footnote immediately above; author's name not given; page given if different from the one preceding
i.e.	*id est:* "that is"; preceded by a comma and followed by a comma and list or explanation
ill., illus.	illustration; illustrated by
l., ll.	line(s)
loc. cit.	*loco citato:* "in the place cited"; refers to work fully identified in any previous footnote except the one immediately preceding; preceded by author's last name; never followed by a page number because *loc. cit.* means "in the same location" (page) as in last footnote referring to that source
MS (MSS)	manuscript(s); always capitalized; no period
N.B.	*nota bene:* "take notice; mark well"; always capitalized
n.d.	no date given
no., nos.	number(s)
n.p.	no place of publication (and/or no publisher) given
op. cit.	*opere citato:* "in the work cited"; preceded by author's last name and followed by page number (because *op. cit.* stands for title only); refers to work cited previously but not immediately above
p., pp.	page(s)
passim	"throughout the work, here and there"; (p. 37 *et passim* means p. 37 and other scattered pages; or pp. 37-42 *passim*)
pl., pls.	plate(s)

pseud.	pseudonym, pen name (Lewis Carroll, Mark Twain)
q.v.	*quod vide:* "which see"
rev.	review by; revised or revised by; revision
sc.	scene
sec., secs.	section(s)
sic	"thus"; not an abbreviation; used within brackets to indicate that an error in quote is in the original: "It was to [*sic*] bad."
st.	stanza
tr., trans.	translator, translation, translated by
v., vv.	verse(s)
viz.	*videlicet:* "namely"; use with or without a period; usage varies
vol., vols.	volume(s); capitalize only before Roman numeral: Vol. VII; 9 vols.

Roman numerals

I	V	X	L	C	D	M
1	5	10	50	100	500	1000

To read a number with two or more Roman numerals, start with the larger numeral and subtract what is to the left; add what is to the right.

If a numeral is between two of greater value, subtract it from the second and then add that number (the remainder) to the first:

$$MCMLXXI = 1971$$

A bar over a numeral multiplies it by 1000. Roman numerals may be written in capitals or in lower case.

$$IX = 9 \quad XXXII = 32 \quad XL = 40 \quad CL = 150$$
$$CD = 400 \quad CDV = 405$$
$$DC = 600 \quad CM = 900 \quad \overline{IV} = 4000$$

Use Roman numerals in capitals (IV, XII, CDL) when you want

> to indicate volumes of books in series;
> to number the acts in a play;
> to number the books of a long poem (or tne cantos);
> to identify different people with the same name (George III);
> to indicate major divisions in an outline;
> to number chapters in the Bible.

Use Roman numerals in lower case (ii, iv, xii) when you want

> to number all prefatory pages including outline and table of contents;
> to identify scenes in a drama;
> to identify verses of chapters in the Bible.

Index